Introduction to
COMPUTER-AIDED
DRAFTING

Introduction to
ER-AIDED DRAFTING

DONALD D. VOISINET

Professor of Technology
Niagara County Community College Sanborn, New York

GREGG DIVISION   McGRAW-HILL BOOK COMPANY

New York Atlanta Dallas St. Louis San Francisco
Auckland Bogotá Guatemala Hamburg Johannesburg
Lisbon London Madrid Mexico Montreal New Delhi
Panama Paris San Juan São Paulo Singapore Sydney
Tokyo Toronto

Sponsoring Editor: **Myrna Breskin**
Editing Supervisor: **Sharon Emily Kaufman**
Design and Art Supervisor/Cover and Interior
Design: **Patricia Frances Lowy**
Production Supervisor: **Priscilla Jane Taguer**

Cover Photograph: **Computervision Corporation**

Library of Congress Cataloging in Publication Data

Voisinet, Donald D., date
   Introduction to computer-aided drafting.

   Includes index.
   1. Computer graphics. I. Title.
T385.V64   1983   604.24′028′54   82-25890
ISBN 0-07-067558-9

1 2 3 4 5 6 7 8 9 0 DOCDOC 8 9 0 9 8 7 6 5 4 3

ISBN 0-07-067558-9

CONTENTS

PREFACE

The wide-scale use of the integrated circuit chip in electronics is revolutionizing the way we work and play. It has dramatically changed the mode of worldwide communications at all levels—personal, industrial, and in every facet of modern-day life. It's on our wrist (quartz digital watches). It's used to solve math problems (hand-held calculators). It entertains (video games) and it helps run businesses (computers). These technological changes are affecting many careers. Retraining people and upgrading job skills is now a necessity in many areas. Drafting is in the forefront of the changes. CAD (computer-aided drafting) is fast becoming a very familiar acronym. Any drafter who wants to upgrade job skills must understand CAD and how it affects his or her career. *Introduction to CAD* will help in understanding how the traditional roles of the drafter are changing. The text presents CAD concepts in a logical, straightforward manner. Anyone possessing interest and a basic knowledge of drafting fundamentals will be able to benefit from this text.

This text was not written with any specific machinery in mind. Rather, the reader can learn enough about general concepts to use a variety of machinery. While it would be best to be able to sit down at a machine during the time you use this text, it is not required to understand the material presented here.

The contents of this text include:

- Why computer-aided drafting is used.
- Types of computer-aided drafting equipment.
- Ways computer-aided drafting is used.
- Preparation of engineering drawings by various methods.
- Commonly used equipment from several manufacturers.

Introduction to CAD is not about computer programming. Drafters do not normally have to know how to program. Drafters use prepared programs to assist in creating drawings. This book explains the basic concepts that a drafter or potential drafter needs to know about CAD. Thus, it will serve as an excellent introduction to this topic.

The text will relate the three categories of CAD equipment. These include micro (or home) computers, mini-computer systems, and mainframe host computer systems. The concepts presented will be valuable because CAD will most certainly become a vital part of virtually every drafter's working career in just a few short years.

Donald D. Voisinet

The Concept of Computer-Aided Drafting

1-1 Introduction

The engineering drawing has been an integral part of industry for many years. It is the link between engineering design and manufacturing. Information is quickly communicated to manufacturing in the form of drawings prepared according to prescribed drafting standards. It is said that a picture is worth a thousand words. Actually, a picture is worth much more. The speed of graphic comprehension can approach a rate 50,000 times that of reading.

CAD Definition

An engineering drawing may be prepared by means other than using the conventional tools. Traditionally, drafting instruments have been used to apply lead or ink on vellum or Mylar. The popular alternative now is to prepare the drawing with the aid of a computer. This method is known as *computer-aided drafting* or *computer-aided design and drafting*. It has rapidly replaced the handmade drawing. Computer-aided design and drafting is abbreviated *CAD* or *CADD*. Several other terms are also used. Some of these are:

- Computer-assisted drafting.
- Computer-augmented drafting.
- Computer-automated drafting.

These and other similar terms are used synonymously. They will be abbreviated as CAD throughout this textbook.

1

CAD History

Commercial computer-aided drafting was introduced in 1964, when the International Business Machines Corp. (IBM) made it commercially available. The first *turnkey* (complete) system was made available in 1970 by Applicon Incorporated. Only recently, however, has the dramatic impact of this new technical tool been felt. By the end of 1982, over 4500 systems were being used by United States industry. The revolution is continuing. The market potential is a tenfold increase by the late 1980s. Although the implementation of CAD in the early 1980s was beginning to develop in the large companies, it now has even much more dramatic effects. This is seen in Fig. 1-1. Note the exponential growth rate in the use of computer graphics terminals.

The *C* in *CAD*

The computer, at first, appears to be a mysterious machine. It is actually, however, an electronic device with no brain. Its capability is limited to basic logical functions. These functions must be determined by a human. They must also be fed into the computer by a human. Each function is performed in sequential order. Such functioning allows the machine to be used for addition, subtraction, etc. To perform a process, the functions must be logically ordered.

Fig. 1-1 The boom in computer graphics.

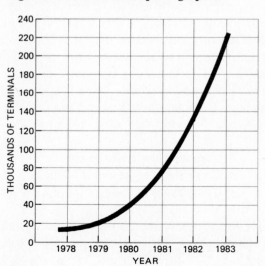

This means that simple events are repeated several times. For example, a multiplication process is conducted as an addition sequence. To multiply 5 × 4, the computer executes 5 + 5 + 5 + 5. The larger the number, the larger the required sequence. The redeeming qualities of the computer lie in the following features.

- The extraordinarily large *number* of functions that can be performed.
- The great *speed* at which each function can be performed.
- The *accuracy* and capacity for repetition of operation.
- The *memory* or *storage* system.

A typical computer terminal is shown in Fig. 1-2.

Computer Programs

A computer's memory enables an individual to program the computer. A *program* includes a written set of detailed instructions. The instructions are set up by a computer programmer. A drafter or designer will normally never need to program. He or she will usually use developed programs. CAD is intended to make the computer accessible to nonprogrammers.

A programmer addresses the computer with a line-by-line format. Each function, or event, is displayed on a horizontal line on the screen. The computer operation and output is limited to the group of functions used. For example purpose only, a partial simple program is shown in Fig. 1-3(a). This program is used to graph-

Fig. 1-2 A sample computer.

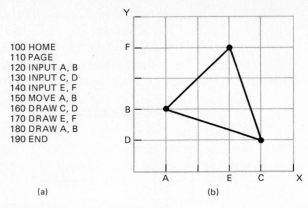

```
100 HOME
110 PAGE
120 INPUT A, B
130 INPUT C, D
140 INPUT E, F
150 MOVE A, B
160 DRAW C, D
170 DRAW E, F
180 DRAW A, B
190 END
```

(a)   (b)

Fig. 1-3 A sample program.

ically display the triangle shown in Fig. 1-3(b). Detailed instructions can also be used to define, analyze, and chart the flow of problems. However, a program that is much more complex than that of Fig. 1-3 would be required to perform such functions. Computer instructions are given in one of several recognized standard languages. The language known as *BASIC* is shown in Fig. 1-3(a). Numerous computer programming courses are available. Course work teaches the programmer methods for preparing any set of detailed instructions. But, again, it is not necessary for a drafter or designer to learn computer programming methods. Numerous programs, known as *software,* exist and are available for use.

The Microprocessor

The advancement in commercially produced microcomputing equipment has led the way in CAD implementation. The term *microminiaturization* refers to the use of integrated circuit (IC) chip technology. This has launched what some have called the technical revolution. Discrete component printed circuit (PC) boards in computers have been replaced by microprocessors (the processing unit of a computer). An example of typical PC and IC components is shown in Fig. 1-4. The PC shown at the top of Fig. 1-4 has been drawn 4 times larger than actual size. The IC pattern, shown at the bottom, appears to be the same size. It is not, however, since it has been drawn 50 times larger than actual size.

The IC chip has made possible the development of microprocessors. The microprocessor fits into small computers giving them a huge capacity. The microprocessor is considered to be the most

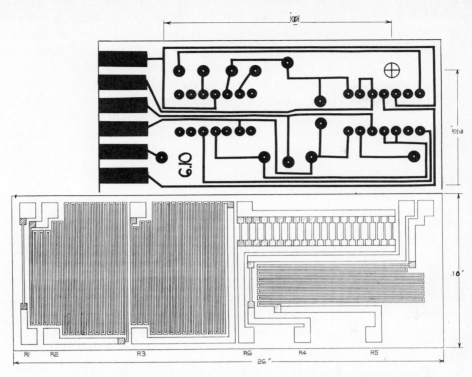

Fig. 1-4 Printed circuit (top) and integrated circuit drawing (bottom).

PC board

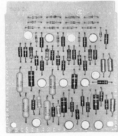

■ IC chip

Fig. 1-5(a) A PC board and an IC chip before packaging.

up-to-date, or state-of-the-art, electronic invention. It contains many times the functional capability of an equivalent-sized transistor PC board. Fig. 1-5(a) shows a comparison between the size of a PC board and an IC chip. The chip, at the bottom, replaces all the resistors (dark cylinders) on the board at the top—at least half of the total number of components. The significant reduction in size is apparent. The size of only the IC chip is shown in Fig. 1-5(a). After the chip has been packaged, it becomes larger, because of the required size of the terminals. But there is still a significant size and weight reduction. Fig. 1-5(b) compares a PC with an IC after packaging.

Cathode-Ray Tube

Another innovation has led to the widespread use of CAD—the development of the graphics display station using a *c*athode-*r*ay *t*ube (CRT). The CRT allows you, the user, to project an image on a screen. The CRT screen resembles a television screen. Its slang

PC board

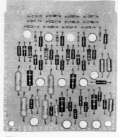

IC chip

Fig. 1-5(b) A PC board and an IC chip after packaging.

1-2 Social Effects

name in industry is the "tube" or "scope." It is the interface between the computer and the computer user, as shown in Fig. 1-6. This interface sets up a two-way (*interactive*) communication. You have control of the unit by the use of an input device. The result of your input is an immediate graphic display of computer calculations. You can then promptly analyze the design or drawing and make a decision about the next step of the process. The procedure may be repeated as many times as necessary. Communication with the computer is not broken. An example of a graphics display is shown in Fig. 1-7. An automobile steering mechanism is displayed on a CRT.

Social aspects of CAD can be devastating to the unfamiliar individual. To make the change from the conventional drafting board to the CRT may cause frustration for several reasons. One primary reason is fear of the unknown. How will this technology affect you as an individual? Deep concern arises as to its effect on your job and your life. Beyond that, human nature generally resists the threat of change.

To help overcome this resistance, industry began introducing CAD as a parallel new system. Traditional methods remained unchanged. Some employees were selected to work on the CRT; others either voluntarily or involuntarily remained on the board. The newer and younger employees were more likely to be selected for the CRT. There were a variety of reasons for this. The most obvious is that they are more easily expended for that task. They have not yet achieved sufficient job experience. Thus, their worth to the company as designers is less. Also, some managements feel, rightly or wrongly, that the younger employee is more innovative and more familiar with computing equipment and, thus, quicker to grasp the CAD concept. This kind of thinking obviously can set up a separation of employees and loom as a threat, particularly to older employees, with regard to job security.

All these concerns will undoubtedly cause problems. In time, they will be solved. Younger employees, for example, will be recognized as having value to the company. It is only through reliance upon them that a company will survive into the future. By the same logic, the company realizes that it is the older employees who possess the experience. They are the backbone of the company. Also, all employees, whether young or old, have the ability to learn.

Courtesy Megatek Corporation

Fig. 1-6 Interactive graphics: computer, CRT, and user.

They will continue to learn new technologies as those technologies emerge. Maintaining a positive attitude is the critical factor. Even those who are reluctant at first lose their inhibitions quickly. Human concern will be further relieved as the separatist philosophy disappears—that is, when the CAD room and the design drafting room become one. This will occur as each designer and drafter acquires a CAD tool.

Fig. 1-7 Automobile steering mechanism displayed on a CRT.

Courtesy Evans & Sutherland Computer Corp., Salt Lake City, Utah

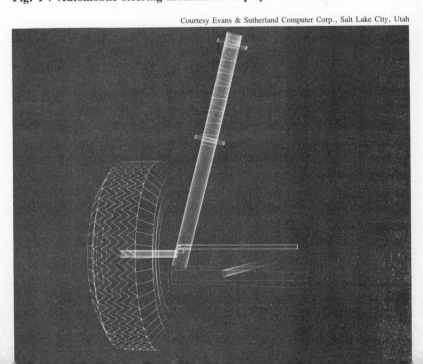

Other social implications involving the use of CAD have emerged. These should be recognized. Because the equipment is state-of-the-art, its use improves company image. A large initial financial outlay for *hardware,* or equipment, is required. For the hardware to be cost effective, higher efficiency is mandated. CAD offers this increased productivity. Pressure on CAD employees to produce more drawings might result. This sometimes makes the individuals possessive of the equipment. At the very least, it puts them on the defensive. A stress situation is likely to be created. Management must strive to alleviate these potential conditions. A motivating and stimulating work environment must be created and maintained. Employees must also understand that it is a higher level of challenge and opportunity that is being offered. Those who understand and accept these factors will become the successful CAD personnel. Remember, as an employee, be enthusiastic and retain a positive attitude.

1-3 System Effects

Positive Aspects of CAD

Computer-aided drafting systems relieve the drafter and designer from tedium. Handmade drawings are no longer required. CAD cannot, however, replace the individual. It cannot think for us. In fact, as earlier stated, computer programmers must instruct computers with considerable detail. A CAD system should be thought of as an additional tool at your disposal. Consider it like a template which helps you to draw more accurately and quickly. The computer is a tool, however, that performs at a high rate of speed. Drawings now can be revised and changed much more quickly and accurately than by hand. Thus, it is economically sound to let it prepare and revise drawings.

Reducing drafting time in a company is of prime importance. The drafting part of a project is considered to be a bottleneck. Traditional industrial drafters spend approximately two-thirds of their time "laying lead." Only one-third is spent for all the other job functions combined—including design. The implementation of CAD changes this. Drawings and design changes can be accomplished much more rapidly. This results in quicker turnaround time. Consequently, projects flow better through a company. The traditional drafting bottleneck is eliminated.

Besides contributing speed, CAD replaces some of the basic techniques that drafters have developed. We do not have to spend endless hours on line weights and lettering. CAD delivers us from tedious and repetitive tasks. CAD thus enhances creativity while it quickly performs the task of showing our ideas. CAD has proven to offer, conservatively speaking, at least a 30 percent time savings in drawing production. This means we can potentially earn at least 30 percent more for our services—assuming, of course, all else is equal.

Drawing creation is still a necessity. CAD primarily replaces only technique to save you time. You will be required to think even more analytically. There will be opportunity for more or additional design options resulting from the extra time. A strong design and drafting background remains essential. Thus, concepts and principles learned in design drafting courses will continue to be important. It is only the time spent developing professional-level technique that is diminished. A somewhat parallel example is the implementation of hand-held calculators. They are used to solve math problems, but knowledge of math is still required by the user to solve problems and calculations must still be made. What is eliminated is the tedious task of performing longhand each mathematical manipulation.

CAD or Traditional Drafting

CAD systems are now mass-produced. Mass production and continued improvement in each new generation of machinery have decreased the cost of CAD systems. Also, software (programs) has been extensively developed, enhancing their adaptability to individual companies' equipment. Thus, virtually every drafter or designer will soon have his or her own CAD unit. This will lessen the impact of the engineering and technical talent shortage. The speed at which mundane tasks are accomplished is greater than ever. Ultimately, extra time will be available to provide the opportunity for more alternative designs to be produced before a final production version is selected. Many firms report no major reduction in project time. More work, however, is done within the same time frame. This additional work is in the form of more designs, more refinement, and more studies. Thus, a better-designed product is the result.

While it may not be practical to handle 100 percent of the workload in a design or drafting office with CAD, all design and drafting most certainly can benefit from CAD. Certain job functions at some companies, however, will continue to be accomplished by traditional means. For example, certain drawings in the construction and electronics fields can be designed more quickly on a drafting board. The time required to enter the information into a CAD system could take too long. Thus, CAD is not necessarily adaptable to every job function. Also, the design process itself is creative, personal, and tends to be secretive. This leads some designers to prefer using their own sketches. This practice, however, may no longer be cost effective. Other factors will depend on product line, company standards, and refinement of the state of the art in computers. Because of these considerations, some companies use CAD for only 25 percent of the workload. Still others approach 100 percent. No matter what the percentage of CAD use, one fact is certain. CAD is having, and will continue to have, dramatic effects on design and drafting careers.

Negative Aspects of CAD

The implementation of CAD systems has great positive value. There are, however, negative aspects to consider. Besides social effects and initial cost, the phenomenon of downtime now exists. *Downtime* means that at certain times you will not be able to use the system. Downtime may be due to the unit's being overloaded by simultaneous requests for use. It also may be due to a component's being out of service. Also, if a component has major problems, the downtime may be extensive. It may last for several hours or even days until a service person can repair the damage. In either case, the traditional drafter would normally not be confronted by this type of situation. Another negative aspect to consider is the potential health hazard. Allegations have been made by some regarding eye damage. Eye damage may be due to the effect of radiation and the flicker rate of the CRT.

Due to the high cost of equipment, many companies have gone to shift work for the designer. The possibility of having to work either the second or third shift is considered by many to be a distinct disadvantage.

**1-4
CAD
Instruction**

Instruction Methods

Once CAD has been installed, the required personnel must be acquired. Trained personnel are obtained from three sources. The first is educational institutions. A multitude of courses and programs are being, or have been, developed by such types of educational institutions as:

- Private schools.
- Vocational schools.
- Community colleges.
- Junior colleges.
- Universities.

They have a variety of offerings to educate drafting students. More and more institutions have obtained equipment. Thus, available educational programs have become commonplace. Also, the cost of mass-produced equipment continues to decrease. Schools with courses and programs are finding it easier to expand their holdings and offerings.

Some schools have not been able to justify the purchase of equipment. This is particularly true of the larger systems. It just is not economically feasible. Some schools have, however, been able to share time with local industries that possess the CAD equipment. The schools are utilizing industry equipment during off hours. Course work is offered to students during these hours. This time-sharing method has several advantages. The school need not purchase costly hardware. The student has an opportunity to learn CAD operation. The student additionally gains familiarity with the industrial setting. The company benefits by improving its community image. Also, it gains an opportunity for early interface with potential future employees.

A second method of acquiring knowledgeable personnel is to train present designers. They may be sent to CAD equipment manufacturer training facilities. These programs were popular during the early days of CAD implementation because trained personnel were virtually impossible to find. This method will have less impact in the future. More and more trained individuals are emerging from educational institutions. These programs will, however, remain as a ''topping off'' experience for employees on a specific manufacturer's equipment.

The remaining popular training method is for the company (employer) to conduct a program using its own facilities. Again, this was popular in the early days because of the shortage of trained personnel. The necessity for the employer to fully train each individual has diminished. Specific instruction peculiar to that company's standards or specific equipment, however, will continue.

Instruction Time

Regardless of how an individual is instructed in the use of CAD, it is best accomplished by an experienced designer. To be competent requires one to spend 3 to 6 months on the equipment. This time period will vary depending on the individual, the type of CAD equipment, and the level of sophistication desired. A minimal level of competency on fairly sophisticated equipment, however, can be developed in a relatively short period of time. A well-developed 1-semester course containing 45 laboratory ("hands on") hours, will produce surprising results. The student normally will be able to produce quite complicated drawings by the course conclusion. After approximately 1 month of actual use following this training, it will take the student, on the average, about the same time to produce a drawing using CAD as it would take that individual at a drafting table. After sufficient experience, it will take the individual, on the average, only one-third as long to produce and revise drawings using CAD as it would take at a drafting table.

Job Title

Once training is completed, the individual becomes a qualified *CAD operator*. This job title is a misnomer for many designers and drafters. The term *operator* is general, and is used to cover all CAD users. Many of the users may not be designers or drafters. It is true, however, that a designer or drafter may be an operator. Consequently, the *CAD operator* title may coincide with *drafter, design drafter,* or *designer,* and the CAD operator should therefore be referred to as such. A drafter becomes a designer after sufficient experience. This promotion varies somewhat from company to company. It does, however, include assuming more and more responsibility. As one definition goes: Designer—when a drafter grows up, that's what she or he becomes.

1-5 Conventional Drafting and CAD

CAD Produces Drawings

For decades, drawings have been produced with pen or pencil. Drawing was accomplished by the hands of a man known as a *draftsman.* As more women entered the profession, the job title slowly evolved into *drafter.* To become a successful drafter, and eventually a designer, the individual first had to develop a thorough knowledge of technical drawing. Next, a level of skill termed *technique* had to be developed. Lastly, study of the theoretical design concepts for an area of specialization was required. The drawings were produced on a traditional drafting table with the aid of hand tools, such as a straight edge, similar to the one shown in the foreground of Fig. 1-8. With the advent of CAD, the traditional drafting table has been, or is being, replaced by a station similar to that shown in the background of Fig. 1-8.

The implementation of CAD has changed the educational requirements for becoming a successful drafter. Programs and curricula that have stressed the development of drafting technique must now revise this practice to survive. As curricula change, the number of students that can be instructed during a lab will also change. Traditional drafting labs normally accommodate 20 to 24 students. With CAD, the lab size is 10 to 12 students and a maximum of 2 per terminal is considered best. A student is seen at a typical interactive work station in Fig. 1-9. Thus, educational institutions must consider more than the initial cost of equipment when revising pro-

Fig. 1-8 Traditional drafting preparation and CAD.

Courtesy IBM Corporation

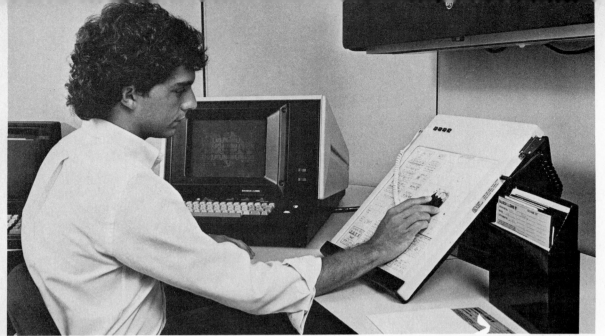

Fig. 1-9 A typical CAD student workstation.

grams. It should be noted that the other two components—technical drawing and theory of design—will continue to be essential. These, coupled with the appropriate mathematics, science, and general education, will continue to produce the well-developed drafter.

Before the adaptation of the computer to CAD, the primary benefit derived from a computer by a designer or drafter was nongraphical output. The computer was used to prepare a program similar to the small example shown in Fig. 1-3(a). A program was prepared with a variety of statements and symbols, and the data was stored in the computer. Various methods were used to accomplish this. Some of the programming languages are FORTRAN, BASIC, PASCAL, ALGOL, C, and COBOL.

As previously indicated, the development of software is accomplished by a computer programmer. Drafters and designers only use programs to prepare designs and drawings. Such programs are much more complicated than the simple example shown in Fig. 1-3(a).

CAD Produces Other Output

The desired drawing or design that is displayed on the CRT screen is converted into a drawing by a CAD system. Not all companies are interested in drawing output. In chemical plant design, for example, liquid- and gas-piping system design requires nongraphic analysis. Thus, some CAD systems are not graphics-based. Other product manufacturing companies also do not always require drawings. Instead, the information is transmitted from the CAD system directly to product manufacturing equipment. This method is known as *CAD/CAM* (*computer-aided design/computer-aided manufacturing*). CAD/CAM increases accuracy since the step of actual drafting preparation where errors may occur is eliminated. The manufacturing equipment may include a wide range of machinery types, such as lathes, milling machines, and so on. The instructions may also be sent to robotic equipment for automatic product handling. CAD/CAM is particularly adaptable to the mechanized segment of industry and is now experiencing dramatic growth.

Segments of Industry

Programs that apply to virtually every segment of industry are available. These include a significant amount of converted mathematical formulas. Design manipulation and analysis are accomplished much more quickly than by traditional methods. The range of tasks that CAD can perform seems to be limited only by the range of programs that can be written.

Segments of industry (and academic disciplines) utilizing CAD, with some sample applications, are given here.

SEGMENT	APPLICATION
Aerospace	Lofting; structural; hydraulics; configuration.
Architectural	Plan views; section elevations; structural; heat loss; plumbing.
Automotive	Kinematics; hydraulics; steering; tires; wiring.
Civil	Mapping; highway; utilities; drain; contour.
Electrical	Control schematics; connection diagrams.
Electronic	Schematic diagrams; PCs; ICs.
Mechanical	Machine design; processes; sheet-metal layout; tooling and fixtures; robotics.
Piping	Single-line schematics; isometric spool diagrams; pressure vessels; petrochemicals; process planning.

The question is no longer *if* the discipline will be converted to CAD, but *when*. In the electronic-electrical areas for example, this has been a foregone conclusion for several years. The companies must have CAD for survival. The recent boom, particularly as applied to CAM and robots, has been in the mechanical discipline. The nature of business in architecture is many small firms and uneven workloads; thus, CAD has arrived somewhat more slowly. It is, however, dominating that field.

Summary

The use of the computer in design and drafting occupations is the most significant engineering development to occur recently. It has hit the technical world like a shock wave, revolutionizing the manner of drawing preparation. This method of producing engineering drawings is known as computer-aided drafting and is commonly referred to as CAD. If the information is to be directly sent to the fabricating machinery, the system is referred to as computer-aided drafting/computer-aided manufacturing (CAD/CAM).

Drawings can be prepared more quickly and accurately with CAD than with traditional methods. Its importance, additionally, lies with:

- Dramatic reduction in turnaround time for changes and revisions.
- Automatic generation of lists (e.g., bill of materials).
- Improvement in the general flow of information throughout a company.

The effect on designers and drafters is dramatic. Retraining of present employees and a change in training for future employees has resulted. Designers, drafters, and engineers have returned to school in droves. Many of the "schools" are not like the traditional ones, however. They include (1) seminars, (2) drafting laboratories, (3) manufacturer locations, (4) informal professional development, and (5) traditional college courses. It has been found that essentially everyone with a positive attitude has been able to adapt to this technological tool. A strong design and drafting background is still necessary to properly operate CAD equipment. Drafting technique, however, has been deemphasized. The machine, which should be considered only a tool, draws and letters for us.

The ultimate effect on the total number of drafting jobs is unclear. What is clear, however, is that drafters will continue to remain an integral component of industry. CAD will enable drafters to be more creative while they spend less time on the more mundane task of "laying lead."

This book will focus on the basic operation of CAD. It will remove the mystery of CAD, whether you possess a system or not. Various hardware manufacturers and types of equipment—large, medium, and small systems—will be described and compared. CAD system operation varies somewhat from unit to unit. The basic goals, however, are common. These will be covered in detail.

Terms to Know

Automation	Equipment that increases productivity without additional expenditure of human energy.
CAD	Computer-aided drafting or computer-aided design and drafting.
CADD	Computer-aided design drafting or computer-aided design and drafting.
CAM	Computer-aided manufacturing.
Chip	A small slice of material (such as silicon) containing electronic devices (transistors, diodes, resistors, and/or capacitors) which perform functions within a computer.
CRT	Cathode-ray tube. Similar to a television screen, this screen allows the production of a drawing (visual display) without the use of vellum or Mylar.
Display	Visual output as seen on the screen of a CRT. It may be a drawing or alphanumeric data.
Hardware	Each piece of physical equipment is considered hardware.
IC	Integrated circuit. See *Chip*.
Interactive	Refers to the need for a human to initiate communication between different parts of a computer system.
Microprocessor	The central processing unit of a microcomputer.
Operator	A general term for CAD users. Not all users are designers and drafters. A designer or drafter, however, may be an operator.
PC	Printed circuit. An electronic assembly comprised of a nonconductive board, a conductive copper pattern, and electronic components.
Program	A detailed set of coded instructions that are logically ordered. These are used for the operation of a computer.

Programmer	An individual who designs the sets of instructions, or programs, for the CAD system.
Software	The name given to programs that are input for the computer. The program gives instructions concerning the operational sequence.
State of the art	Referring to the latest technical advancement.
Traditional drafter	A drafter not trained in CAD whose time is spent on traditional drafting techniques and tasks.
Turnkey	The name given to a complete CAD system.
User	The individual who inputs data into and receives information from a CAD system.

Questions

1. What term is used to describe the transmission of design information directly to manufacturing with the aid of a computer?
2. What is the most popular name for CAD?
3. Why use a computer if a human can accomplish the same task?
4. How is software for a computer prepared?
5. What development has been most responsible for CAD implementation?
6. Virtually any drafter or designer can learn CAD if she or he ——— ?
7. What drafting function is no longer required when CAD is used?
8. What are the important positive aspects of using CAD?
9. What are the important negative aspects of using CAD?
10. How many hours of instruction are necessary for a minimal level of competency with CAD?
11. What is the proper job title for a person who prepares drawings using CAD?
12. What are the increased costs associated with CAD instruction?
13. What segments of industry have been affected by CAD?

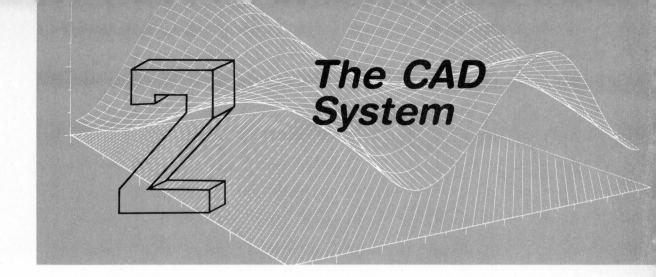

The CAD System

2-1 Composition of a CAD System

Ⓐ CAD system is made up of various combinations of equipment. This holds true for small, medium, and large system applications. The specific package selected largely depends on the needs of the user. Various types of drawings, referred to as *hard copy,* may be preferred by certain companies. Other companies may not require any drawing whatsoever. This means that one company will choose a piece of equipment that prepares a drawing one way. Another company will select equipment that uses another method for preparation of drawings. Still a third company will not utilize any equipment to produce graphic displays or hard copies.

Generally, each piece of equipment can be categorized as one of the following types:

- Processing.
- Input.
- Output.

This chapter will analyze each major piece of equipment that falls within one or overlaps several of these categories. The purpose and function of each piece will be analyzed and its relationship to the complete package will be indicated. Fig. 2-1 shows an overall diagram of a complete system. These are the items present in most applications. The graphic display station and central processing unit (CPU) are considered part of the processing equipment. An alphanumeric (letters and numbers) keyboard is used to manually

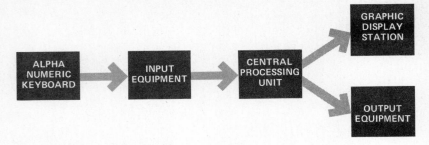

Fig. 2-1 A typical system arrangement.

input data and is normally attached to the graphic display station as one unit. In combination, these units are commonly referred to as a *terminal*. A CPU may be reserved for a single purpose. It is normally attached to the terminal; this combination is commonly referred to as a *computer*.

The typical system arrangement is *interactive*. This means that a person must cause the interaction between the CPU and the graphic display station. An alphanumeric keyboard or other input equipment may aid this process. After the design and/or drawing on the CAD unit has been completed, the information may be transferred to various output devices.

Fig. 2-2(a) shows a system arrangement for one type of setup. The design console is positioned at the right. It includes a graphic display station and keyboard. Also shown at this location is an input device known as a *graphics tablet,* or *digitizer*. An enlarged view of this portion of the equipment is shown in Fig. 2-2(b). The unit located at the center foreground of Fig. 2-2(a) includes the programs and the means to process them. One type of output equipment shown at the left rear of the figure is known as a *plotter*.

2-2 Graphic Display Station

The purpose of the graphic display station is to project an image onto a screen. The image displays data either in an alphanumeric (written) or in graphical (pictorial) manner. The primary use of this device in CAD application is graphical. The user can view a picture of the design as the design is being entered into the system. This display can be accomplished by a variety of ways since many image display devices are available.

(a)

(b)

Fig. 2-2 System equipment setup.

Cathode-Ray Tube

A popular graphic display station is the CRT. The display method is similar to a television screen. Screen displays are shown in Fig. 2-3. Fig. 2-3(a) and (b) shows a wire frame image of a bench grinder on a CRT. Another CRT display, known as a *dual display*, is shown in Fig. 2-3(c). The common types of CRTs are described here.

Vector. The vector writing CRT is drawn on by an X-Y direction coordinate system. This is similar in principle to the popular Etch a Sketch toy. The computer first locates points, then connects the points in a way similar to the following format.

POINT LOCATION	POINT CONNECTION
A @ X_A, Y_A	—
B @ X_B, Y_B	A to B
C @ X_C, Y_C	B to C

The above table is interpreted as follows: first, point A will be located at a horizontal (X) and vertical (Y) coordinate position. Next, point B will be located in exactly the same manner. These point positions (A and B) are then connected. Next, point C is located and then connected to B, and so on. Other names given to

(a)

Courtesy Lexidata Corporation

(b)

Courtesy Lexidata Corporation

Courtesy Calma Company, a wholly owned subsidiary of the General Electric Company, U.S.A.

(c)

Fig. 2-3(a) High-resolution image. (b) Low-resolution image. (c) Dual CRT display.

this method are *stroke writing* and *calligraphic writing*. The process by which vector images are written is known as *refresh*. Each line in the picture is rewritten so that it appears steady to the observer. Thus, an image is vector-refreshed with each change.

Raster. Raster differs from vector in how displayed data is represented. The *raster* type uses a grid network to display the image. This is similar to the standard television screen display. Each grid is either a dark or a light image that falls within a square area that appears on the screen as a dot. Each dot is known as a *pixel*. An analogy for how this works is a placard pattern used by fans in the stands of a football game. The cards are used to show a graphical message, and each fan within the pattern holds up either a dark or a light card. At a sufficient distance, the combinations of dark and light spots produce a recognizable image. This phenomenon is shown by the arrow in Fig. 2-4.

The *resolution* (clearness) of a raster-developed image will depend on the closeness of lines forming the grid pattern. The smaller the pixels, the more resolution the image has. The greater the number of dots per unit area, the greater the resolution. The greater number of dots improves picture quality. For example, a blown-up photograph has a loss in resolution, or clearness because of the reduced number of dots per unit area. There is almost an unlimited amount of picture information available with raster scan. This eliminates uneven jogged lines (known as *jaggies*) produced by other image display devices. An example of a low-resolution (jaggy) display is shown in Fig. 2-3(b). Note the difference in resolution between (a) and (b) in Fig. 2-3. Figure 2-3(a) illustrates higher resolution. The intensity of light in each pixel of a raster system can be controlled. By varying the intensity, shadows can be produced for a more realistic image.

Raster display is quickly accomplished by the refresh method. The complete image is redrawn at a rate of speed exceeding the human grasp. The picture is refreshed, or scanned, from left to right and from top to bottom very rapidly. When comparing it to the vector method, remember, "Raster does it faster."

Storage Tube. A storage tube allows a line to be plotted without the use of the refresh method. A phosphor surface on the tube is bombarded by electrons to produce the image. Some storage tubes have the ability to hold the image steady without flicker. A line is

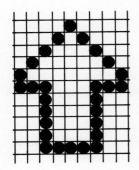

Fig. 2-4 Raster display on a CRT.

added by the addition of electrons based on a command by the user. A single line, however, cannot be deleted. The entire screen must be erased and redrawn (*repainted*). This requires additional time.

Color. The types of CRTs mentioned so far produce the image in one color, similar to the conventional black and white television. Any raster refresh system can be color-enhanced quite readily by the use of three electron guns rather than one. This display screen is similar to the common color television screen. Each gun emits one of the primary television colors: red, green, or blue. From combinations of these, any color pattern may be set up. The vast majority of new graphic display stations marketed will contain this option, except storage tubes, which are limited to one color.

Other Displays

There are several other types of graphic display stations. They are less popular and will not be likely to replace the CRT types.

The first type is plasma. *Plasma* technique uses a flat, thin panel and the glow from an inert gas to display the image. Neon is the gas commonly used. The gas is ionized to emit visible light in a matrix dot pattern. The plasma technique is potentially popular since it is better for your eyes than the CRT. The CRT has low-level radiation emission and a flicker associated with it. These may possibly pose a health hazard over an extended period of time. This health hazard possibility is eliminated with the plasma panel display which is virtually flicker-free and will not "squirt electrons in your face." The primary disadvantage of plasma display is that it produces poor resolution. Also, the size of the panel is small.

Other types of graphic display stations include electro-illuminescent, liquid crystal, and projection techniques. Each has its associated problems, and their use is much less extensive than that of the CRT.

2-3
Keyboard

The alphanumeric keyboard allows you to communicate with the CPU. It is used to manually input data. The primary use of the keyboard is for nongraphic work. The keyboard resembles a standard typewriter as shown in Fig. 2-5. *Alpha* refers to the keys that input letters of the alphabet. *Numeric* refers to the other keys, each of which inputs a number. The user may type in an alphanumeric

Courtesy Tektronix, Inc.

Courtesy Adage, Inc.

Fig. 2-5 Alphanumeric keyboards.

instruction. Input is completed by pressing the carriage return (or some similar key). Since computers have become so popular, knowledge of the keyboard is indispensable for anyone involved with CAD. The speed of inputing data with the keyboard is a function of the ability to use the keyboard. Thus, users will benefit greatly by taking an introductory typing course. Remember, time is valuable.

The alphanumeric keyboard is normally combined with a CRT. This terminal enables the operator to immediately see each manual instruction on the display screen.

2-4 Central Processing Unit

The central processing unit (CPU) is the computing portion of the system. Commonly, it is referred to as the computer. A multitude of integrated circuit (IC) chips are combined together. These allow the performance of fundamental computations. The number of computations, or the capacity of the unit, is designated by the number of bytes. *Byte* is the base term used by the system manufacturers. It describes a character of memory containing 8 bits.

A *bit* is a binary digit. All messages are sent to a microprocessor by means of the binary code—a two-digit system using the symbols 1 and 0. The digit 1 refers to the presence of a signal (on). The digit 0 refers to the lack of a signal (off). A two-digit signal is transmitted by the operator whenever a key is pressed on the alphanumeric keyboard. Sixteen and thirty-two bit machines are becoming more commonly available. A 16- or 32-bit machine can process two or four characters of information at one time. A character of information may be either a letter or a number. No matter if the unit is an 8-, a 16-, or a 32-bit type, the basic unit will be a byte. Thus, a 32K-byte unit will have a capacity of approximately 32,000 characters of memory.

The size of the CPU will determine the size of the CAD system. *Micro unit* is used for small systems; *mini unit* for medium systems; and *mainframe unit* for large systems.

Micro System

The micro unit, used for small applications, has a typical memory capacity in the 16K to 64K range. This means there is enough space to store about 16,000 to 64,000 characters. The micro unit will normally be combined with a graphic display station and an alphanumeric keyboard as one unit (shown in Fig. 2-6). This unit is known as a *desk-top computer*.

Fig. 2-6 A sample computer.

Courtesy Apple Computer, Inc.

Micro systems are economically priced. Consequently, they are often used for initial data entry. Although their capacity is small, much work can be accomplished with them. Thus, large expensive systems need not be tied up with preliminary work. The data gathered on the micro can later be transferred to a larger system. This procedure will be further outlined in Chap. 5.

Mini Systems

A unit in this category is generally referred to as a *stand-alone,* turnkey, or *dedicated* system. Stand-alone equipment refers to a unit that can process the data fed into it without having to address a mainframe or separate CPU. More than one terminal may be part of the system. The mini system is somewhat similar to the micro system but with added capability. It has a greater memory capacity and normally is 32-bit as opposed to 8-bit. Thus, it falls between the micro and the mainframe in both capability and cost. These turnkey systems constitute the majority of the CAD systems used today.

Mainframe

The mainframe is a large CPU (or *host* computer) possibly consisting of as many as several million memory characters. The mainframe is utilized for a multitude of functions. It offers more capability and is configured differently than the micro and mini systems. It was also available long before CAD became popular. Thus, it was the most popular type during the early days of CAD. Mainframe terminals are normally found in a remote location of the workplace and are not combined into one unit as is the micro system. For example, several terminals, each of which may be in a remote location (physically near neither another terminal nor the CPU), are still connected to the same processing unit. This is schematically shown in Fig. 2-7.

2-5 Software

Program Language

Software includes written sets of instructions (programs) that are used to input information into the system. Programs are written in a variety of languages. The most common of these is known as FORTRAN (*FOR*mula *TRAN*slation). Another common language is

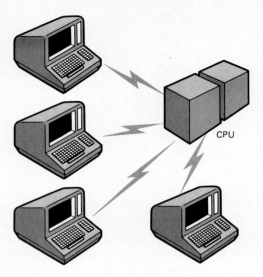

Fig. 2-7 A mainframe system.

BASIC (*B*eginners *A*ll-purpose *S*ymbolic *I*nstruction *C*ode). BASIC is popular since it uses English-like and math-like "easy-to-use" language. The notations are made up of statements rather than sentences. There are several versions of BASIC. One version is illustrated by the small example program shown in Fig. 1-3. Some other high-level program languages are COBOL (*CO*mmon *B*usiness-*O*riented *L*anguage), ALGOL (*ALGO*rithmic *L*anguage), PASCAL, APL, and C. These, however, are not common to CAD.

No matter which language is used, drafters and designers need not necessarily develop a knowledge of them. Some proficiency, however, may be desired and introductory programming courses may be taken for this purpose.

The drafter or designer will normally serve as the *user* of programs rather than the *developer*. Consequently, the programs will be received complete. Software has been extensively developed over the years. A medium-sized series will be likely to exceed an investment of 500 work hours in a program. This means that one computer programmer has spent over 500 hours of his or her time. The variety of programs available depends on the manufacturer or vendor. With over 800 software vendors on the market, it is not surprising that an extensive listing is available. The recommendation with software is "Buy—don't build." If the desired software to do the job can be purchased, why invest up to 500 work hours to develop a new program? Also, if you build it, it's yours. You must maintain it, update it, etc. This maintenance becomes a waste of time and is often difficult.

Storage

Small- and medium-sized CAD systems will normally store programs on a *disk* or *cassette*. The primary storage media is the disk, also referred to as a *diskette*. The programs are stored magnetically on a plasticlike (Mylar) surface. A cassette, while much less popular, may also be used. It is similar to an 8-track audio cassette. An illustration of a cassette is shown in Fig. 2-8(a). Several programs may be contained on each cassette. In that event, a directory will be included with the cassette. Each program will be listed by number and title. You may easily select a program by pressing the corresponding keyboard number. After the program has been selected, it may take "minutes" to find the program. This time lag is a disadvantage of the cassette.

A disk, or diskette, will economically store programs plus offer high-speed retrieval. Only "seconds" are required to find a program. A program may be found in one of two ways—by the *sequential* method or the *random* method. Sequential retrieval means that you retrieve information in order starting at the beginning. The random method allows information to be retrieved or entered immediately. This is commonly referred to as *direct access*. It is accomplished by designating two or more sections on the disk. When you specify the section number, the data is immediately found. Search time is not required. Thus, sequential retrieval is quick but random is immediate. Methods to enter and retrieve data using a disk will be analyzed in Chap. 5.

Different types of disks are available. There are hard types and flexible types. Disks are also known as single or dual. This means that data storage may be one-sided (*single*) or that data may be on both sides (*dual*) of the disk. A flexible disk is similar in appearance to a 45-rpm phonograph record. It is, however, thinner. Also, since it is made from Mylar, it is more flexible. Hence, the term *floppy* disk. Two standard diameters for floppy disks are 5.5 in and 8 in. These are illustrated in Fig. 2-8(b) and (c). Note the protective covering over the larger disk. Disks must be handled gently. Even a small scratch can ruin the contents of the disk. The

Courtesy Tektronix, Inc.

(a)

(b)

Courtesy Tektronix, Inc.

(c)

Fig. 2-8(a) A tape cartridge. (b) An unprotected floppy disk. (c) A floppy disk with protective cover.

cover will protect the disk from dust, dirt, and accidental scratching. It cannot, however, prevent mishandling. A disk, for example, cannot be used for a Frisbee or exposed to heat or magnetic fields. The contents will almost immediately become useless.

Notice the small tab located on the lower-right portion of the protective covering. This is used to protect disk contents. It is possible to accidentally write over the data on the disk with new data. The original data is then destroyed. The small tab covers a hole in order to prevent this. This safety procedure is known as *write protect*.

Hard, or rigid, disks are available in various configurations. They normally can handle a larger amount of data than a floppy disk. Winchester is one type used with some CAD systems. This disk is sealed in a container. Thus, in addition to having a greater capacity, it is also more durable than the floppy. In general, a comparison of the hard to the flexible disk shows the hard disk:

- Performs better.
- Has greater capacity.
- Is more durable.
- Is more expensive.

The larger CAD units, containing a mainframe system, utilize a different software format. The programs are stored on disks and magnetic tapes. They are however a different type, providing extended capability over the small and medium-sized systems. As in all computer instructions, the language of electrical impulses (the binary system) is used. Each portion of a program will normally represent a particular function. The functions are combined in the preparation of an engineering drawing. For example, one part will instruct the machine to draw a line, another part a circle, and so on. After each function has been programmed, they are combined. In the designing or preparation of a drawing on the CRT, the desired function is *recalled*. The recall may be accomplished by another piece of equipment, known as a *function board*, which will be studied in the next section.

Software can be developed in virtually any graphical configuration. Also, as previously noted, some CAD systems are non-graphic-based. The software used for these systems, thus, must be different. This means that more than an engineering drawing can be prepared on the CRT screen. Any sort of chart, graph, design data, design analysis, and so on, can be programmed. The limit is determined by the skill of the software developer and the size of the computer. An example of other sort of data that can be represented is shown in Fig. 2-9.

2-6 Function Board

The term *function board* describes a piece of input equipment that is used to retrieve a program or part of a program. A function board contains several buttons, keys, or sensing elements. Each part of the program is connected to one of the buttons, keys, or sensing elements, and these are operated during the execution of a particular function. A function board is referred to differently by various manufacturers. Some of the names given to this device are:

- Program function keyboard.
- Function keyboard.
- Program board.
- Command board.
- Menu pad.
- Menu tablet.

Fig. 2-9 A three-dimensional design analysis.

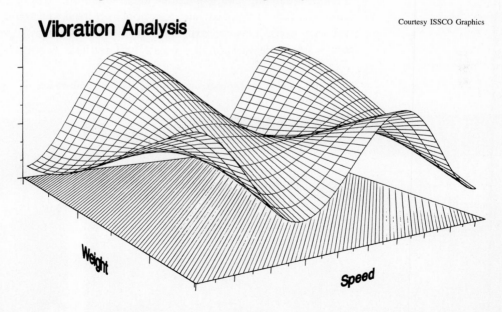

Courtesy ISSCO Graphics

Vibration Analysis

Weight

Speed

The term *program function keyboard* is probably the most descriptive. For simplicity, however, the term *function board* will be used to describe any which have buttons or keys. Also, to avoid confusion, the term *button* will be used in discussions of the function board. The term *key* will be reserved for reference to the alphanumeric keyboard.

The arrangement of the buttons varies with the hardware manufacturer. Some of the smaller dedicated units combine buttons directly on the alphanumeric board of the computer. An example of this is shown in Fig. 2-10 at the left. The buttons located to the upper left of Fig. 2-10(a) have been designated as *user-definable keys* (UDK) by the manufacturer. The 10 buttons actually have 20 selections because of the uppercase-lowercase shift key (as on a standard typewriter). Small CAD menu boards may have as few as 10 commands, whereas a large system may have as many as several hundred.

Manufacturers of larger mini systems have a completely separate board, illustrated in Fig. 2-11. Each of the particular functions associated with the corresponding button may be identified. The functions vary depending on what may be accomplished by a particular system. Figure 2-11 represents a typical medium-sized board. Other systems may retrieve functions in a different manner. One such type is shown in Fig. 2-12. Rather than buttons, the board contains a sensing element under each selection. These types of buttonless function boards are commonly referred to as *menu pads*. Each command may be expressed in either alphabet or graphical form. Any selection on the board will retrieve a portion of the

Fig. 2-10(a) Program buttons on computer. (b) Thumbwheels on computer.

(a)

Courtesy Tektronix, Inc.   (b)

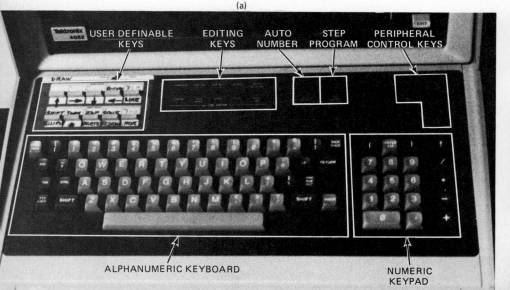

USER DEFINABLE KEYS   EDITING KEYS   AUTO NUMBER   STEP PROGRAM   PERIPHERAL CONTROL KEYS

ALPHANUMERIC KEYBOARD

NUMERIC KEYPAD

program corresponding to the desired title or symbol. Often, a menu limits the design drafter to only certain types of schematic diagrams. Both the software and the menu, however, can be changed on many of these systems. One way is to insert different tapes or disks. Completely different applications are thus programmed into the unit. A different menu card, or *mask*, corresponding to a particular program may be placed over the buttons. A menu card is a thin plastic card similar to the one shown in Fig. 2-13.

Fig. 2-11 Separate program function keyboard.

Fig. 2-12 Menu pad.

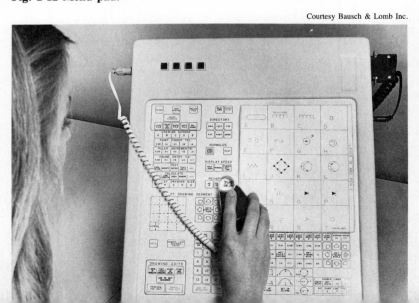

Courtesy Koh-I-Noor Rapidograph, Inc.

Fig. 2-13 Menu card or mask.

2-7 Processing Memory

Additional devices are required to allow input to or output from the processing equipment. Among those required are the drives and memories. The smaller systems, which use disk or tape cassettes, require equipment to drive the software. A disk drive may also be referred to as an operating system. It receives the flexible disk directly as shown in Fig. 2-14 and may be used as permanent storage. The information on the disk may be a program. It may also be used for other purposes such as a directory to maintain files, etc. Some systems utilize two disk drives: one contains the programs; the other is used to maintain a permanent record of drawings after they have been developed. The disk drive itself is a piece of hard equipment. A packaged program known as a file manager or disk driver is software. In the less likely event that tape cassettes are used in the system, a tape drive is used. The tape drive enables data storage and retrieval to occur. The unit may be a separate piece of equipment, or it may be part of the computer as shown in Fig. 2-15.

Fig. 2-14 Loading a flexible disk in a drive.

Courtesy Bausch & Lomb Inc.

Fig. 2-15 Tape drive as part of a computer.

Computers must have *memory* systems to store programs and data. The memory may be either permanent or temporary. Permanent memory is referred to as *read-only memory* (ROM). Temporary memory is referred to as *random access memory* (RAM). RAM provides temporary storage locations for entries made by any input device, allowing a program to be developed. Each entry that is made must conform to the correct program language. The statement is entered first into the CPU and then to a RAM location. The complete set of statements (or program), up to system capacity, are stored in RAM. Data flow to and from RAM is controlled by the CPU. The statements are executed sequentially whenever proper direction is given. The result is displayed on the CRT. The contents of a program on a disk can also be loaded in RAM.

The contents of RAM are always destroyed when the power supply to the system is removed. ROM, however, is not affected by the interruption of power flow. Also, the contents of RAM are constantly being updated. Thus, it is known as temporary storage. The tape or disk unit provides the permanent data storage. The CPU is the main device that directs all operations. Various devices input information directly to the CPU. The RAM and tape or disk drive either input data to the CPU or receive output from it. This setup is shown in Fig. 2-16. CAD system capability is enhanced by several other peripheral input and output devices. A *peripheral* is an additional piece of equipment that may be used in conjunction with the computer. Peripherals will be covered in subsequent sections of this chapter.

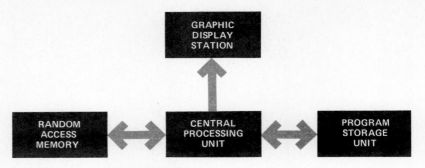

Fig. 2-16 Design console memory setup.

2-8 Graphics Tablet

Digitizing

A graphics tablet is an input device. In terms of graphics, it is far more important than the keyboard. Also, it has many purposes. One use is quick and accurate graphic conversion. A rough sketch can be converted to a finished drawing by the transferring of point and line locations to the CRT screen. Information is based on the X-Y (horizontal-vertical) line coordinate system. It is entered quickly and efficiently into the computer, using this so-called "electronic drawing board" (the graphics tablet). The result of the input data is graphically displayed on a CRT. This method is commonly known as *digitizing*. Consequently, a graphics tablet is referred to as a *digitizer*. The keyboard also cannot input graphical symbols. This can readily be accomplished by digitizing.

Several pieces of equipment are used in conjunction with the graphics tablet. These may include a stylus or pen, a push-button cursor or puck, a power module or console, and a menu. The tablet itself is a flat surface and is available in a wide range of sizes. It may vary from a small surface area accommodating A-size drawings (9 in × 12 in or 228 millimeters [mm] × 304 millimeters [mm]) to one which exceeds E-size drawing area. (36 in × 48 in or 910 mm × 1220 mm). Beneath the surface lies a grid pattern of many horizontal and vertical lines. These lines are used to detect electrical pulses at desired X-Y coordinate locations using a stylus or puck. Their locations are transferred to the computer. Figure 2-17(a) illustrates a small tablet with an associated stylus. Figure 2-17(b) illustrates a larger tablet using a push-button puck.

Puck and Stylus

The position of each desired point of a drawing or sketch on the tablet is sensed by a puck or stylus. Several styles of pucks and

(a)   Courtesy Adage, Inc.

(b)   Courtesy Bausch & Lomb Inc.

Fig. 2-17(a) Graphics tablet and stylus. (b) Graphic tablet and puck.

styluses are available. Figure 2-18 illustrates a few variations. The pucks are (from the left) 4-button, 13-button, and single-button models.

Each has fine black cross hairs that are used for positioning. Pressing the appropriate button causes horizontal (X) and vertical (Y) data to be sent quite accurately to the computer by an electrical signal. The result is displayed on the CRT screen as a bright mark. This method, known as *digitizing,* may be repeated as often as necessary to complete the drawing.

Different puck configurations operate differently. For example, the 4-button cursor shown in Fig. 2-18 operates as follows:

- The button located farthest from the cross hair is pressed to start a sequence.
- The button located farthest left is pressed to verify a location.
- The button located nearest the cross hair is pressed to place into memory (RAM) the information.
- The button located farthest right is pressed to end the sequence.

The power module shown in Fig. 2-19 not only supplies power but also allows the unit to operate in various modes. For example, the operational mode known as the POINT mode has just been discussed. A single X-Y coordinate pair is available by either a stylus touch-down or a push of a button on a puck. Another operational mode known as the STREAM mode can be selected to update coordinate pairs continuously. Thus, a continuous line can be drawn on the CRT screen.

Tablet Menu

Many graphic tablets are provided with a menu that contains a variety of commands. The menu may appear on the screen, or it may be placed on the tablet. A menu placed directly on the tablet is shown in Fig. 2-20. The menu normally will occupy only a minor

Fig. 2-18 Puck and stylus.

Courtesy Summagraphics Corporation

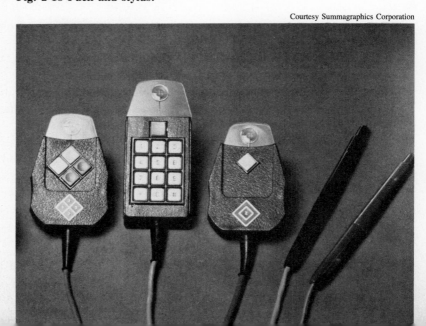

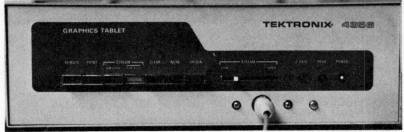

Fig. 2-19 Graphic tablet console.

Fig. 2-20 Digitizing a graphics tablet menu item.

portion of the tablet surface area. The location varies with each manufacturer. The main purpose on all systems, however, is rapid data conversion. A symbol, for example, may be generated off the menu by the use of the stylus or puck. You can accomplish this by pointing to the menu item and touching down. Next, signal the desired position on the graphics tablet. The result is displayed on the CRT screen. The process is repeated until the drawing, as displayed on the CRT, is finished. A CAD system illustrating the pieces of equipment covered thus far is shown in Fig. 2-21.

Fig. 2-21 CAD system.

2-9 Light Pen

A light pen is used as an input pointing device. It is also considered a digitizer since it can change displayed points on the CRT screen. Pens are lightweight; however, this is not the reason for the name *light pen*. The pen is electric and contains a photocell sensory element. Hence the term *light pen*. Attached to one end is a cable through which the signal is transmitted. The other end of the pen may be positioned by hand to a desired screen location. After positioning, touch the screen with the tip of the pen. Depressing it causes the pen to become activated. Light spots are sensed. A signal is sent to the system indicating the position. By this method, any element of the graphic display may be identified to the computer. One disadvantage of the light pen occurs with prolonged use. After several hours a drafter may tire from holding the pen. Beyond that, however, the light pen functions quite well.

The light pen is moved about the display screen and indicates the current position under consideration. The position is illuminated by a blinking character (rectangle, arrow, or cross hair) or an extra bright spot. This indicating position is referred to as a *cursor*. Do not confuse this with the puck sometimes used with a graphics tablet. Some graphics tablet manufacturers refer to the puck as a cursor. This causes confusion. In this text, the term *cursor* will always refer to the indicating position on the CRT screen.

If a light pen is not used, other means, such as the double thumbwheels shown at the right of Fig. 2-10, are used to move the cursor. Normally, one thumbwheel allows movement in the X direction and the other in the Y direction. Another method of cursor control is by means of a joystick.

2-10 Joystick

Fig. 2-22 A joystick.

Courtesy Adage, Inc.

Direction Control

A *joystick* is another type of device used to control the cursor. It can be added to many systems, further enhancing CAD capability. The joystick shown in Fig. 2-22 is simply an extended version of the type commonly seen with video games. An electrical connection to the computer is made with a cable. The joystick steers a lighted cursor on the console screen. The cursor provides visual feedback to the user and is positioned in the X-Y axis. In other words, the joystick points the cursor to a location by an electrical signal through wires.

A command is executed by tilting the joystick lever. This lever extends vertically through the top of the unit shown in Fig. 2-22. The tilt angle, looking down on the unit (plan view), determines the direction of cursor movement. Think of the direction as being in a 360° circular pattern. Starting with 0° towards the horizontal right (east or three o'clock), the rotation direction is counterclockwise. Thus, to move the cursor position left or right horizontally, tilt the stick either to the left (180°) or right (0°). For vertical movement, tilt it either directly up (90°) or down (270°). Any combination of X and Y movements can be made with a corresponding tilt of the stick.

Speed Control

The rate of speed at which the cursor is moved on the screen is variable. It is proportional to the distance that the stick is moved from the vertical position. Another way to think of this is to consider the angle that the stick makes with the horizontal as seen in an elevation view of the joystick. In the vertical position (90° angle), there is essentially no cursor movement. As the joystick is tilted (less than 90°), the cursor begins to move. The greater the tilt, the smaller the angle with the horizontal and the greater the rate of cursor movement. The cursor movement is not exactly nonexistent with the stick in the vertical position. There may be a very slow movement, depending on equipment manufacturer. This phenomenon is known as *drift*.

Use

A joystick is a handy device for certain functions, for example, creation of general symbol shapes, which may be too cumbersome to perform with other processing controls. With a joystick, shapes are very rapidly created. Alternately move the cursor position to quickly draw lines. A disadvantage of joystick positioning is control difficulty. It is not useful for high accuracy applications. If an accurate symbol drawn to size must be generated, the joystick cannot be used. More likely, the coordinates would need to be keyed in exactly using alphanumeric data. The user would then need to tediously input each individual X and Y coordinate for each point. The methods used to perform such operations as coordinate input will be covered in Chap. 3.

2-11 Pen Plotter

A line-type digital plotter is an electromechanical graphics output device. This unit, shown in Fig. 2-23, is capable of moving a pen in two dimensions across paper media. Because of incremental movement, a plotter is considered a vector device. The main use of the plotter is to produce an image of the CRT graphic display. This can be any combination of lines and alphanumerics. If a CAD system is thought of as an automated drafting machine, the plotter is the part replacing the activity of "laying lead."

Ink pens normally are used to produce a permanent copy of a drawing. Various types of pens can be used, such as wet ink, felt tip, or liquid ball. They may be a single color, as shown in Fig. 2-24(a) and (b), or multicolor, like that in Fig. 2-24(c). Different pens are inserted or removed rather quickly. A common way is by a quarter-turn twist. One such pen is shown in Fig. 2-24(a). The pens will draw on various types of media. Most popular are vellum and Mylar (polyester film). Also, such items as color overhead transparency stock may be used. Being able to match the medium to its purpose is a distinct advantage of the digital plotter. Another advantage is that the drawing produced is of high quality and is

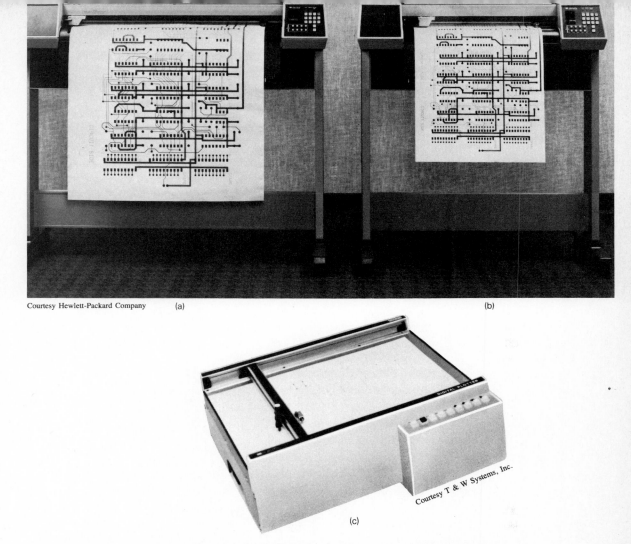

Courtesy Hewlett-Packard Company   (a)   (b)

Courtesy T & W Systems, Inc.

(c)

Fig. 2-23(a) and (b) Microgrip pen plotters. (c) Flatbed pen plotter.

uniform and precise. On the other hand, it is expensive. Consequently, this type of copy tends to be permanent. Prints are made from it, and it is the most dominant means of producing a final CAD drawing.

The pen plotter is slow compared to other output devices. It will take from several seconds (simple drawing) to several minutes (complex drawing) to produce a copy—a disadvantage for a user requiring large-scale production. Yet, pen plotters will remain the most common output device for low- to medium-volume applica-

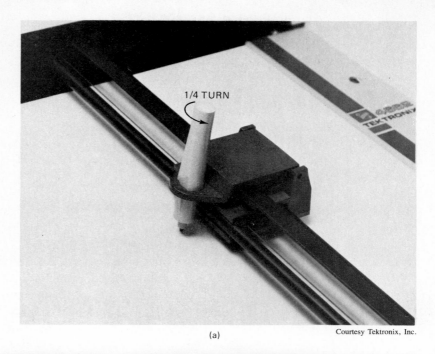

1/4 TURN

(a)   Courtesy Tektronix, Inc.

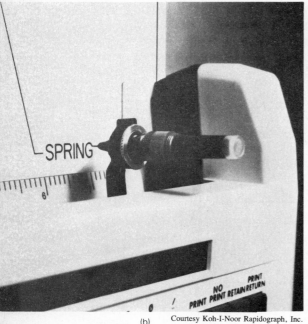

SPRING

6

NO   PRINT
PRINT PRINT RETAIN RETURN

(b)   Courtesy Koh-I-Noor Rapidograph, Inc.

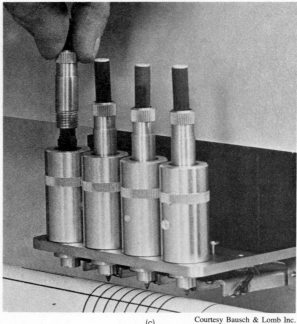

(c)   Courtesy Bausch & Lomb Inc.

Fig. 2-24(a) and (b) Single pen plotter. (c) Multi pen plotter.

tions. This still represents a major reduction of time from traditional hand methods of producing these drawings.

Pen plotter technology includes the drum, microgrip, and flatbed types.

- *Drum.* A drum plotter consists of a long narrow cylinder and a pen carriage. The surface area is curved rather than flat and is in the shape of a cylinder. Hence the term *drum*. The drum rotates to provide one axis of movement. The carriage moves the pen(s) to provide the other axis of movement.
- *Microgrip.* The medium is gripped at the edges with a microgrip plotter. The paper is moved back and forth. High performance is attained at a low cost. Popular microgrip plotters are illustrated in Fig. 2-23(a) and (b).
- *Flatbed.* Pen movement occurs in both axes with the flatbed plotter. The pen carriage is controlled both in the X axis and Y axis. Motors and cable are used for control. Short digital steps, normally less than 0.010 in long, produce the line. The vellum, Mylar, or other medium is loaded on the bed surface by electrostatic attraction. A typical flatbed plotter is shown in Fig. 2-23(c).

The surface area of a pen plotter, as with the graphics tablet, may be as small as an A size yet larger than an E size. Also, the size of the drawing to be placed on the paper can vary. You are able to vary the scale of the lines and characters manually by setting the plotting surface area. Normally, the lower left-hand corner and upper right-hand corner are set as the boundaries. This may be done with a joystick built into the machine. It controls the plotter pen in the manner described in Sec. 2-10. Instead of cursor movement control, however, a pen carriage is controlled.

2-12 Hard Copy Unit

A hard copy duplicates the CRT display quickly and conveniently. The primary advantage of this technique is that of speed. It produces output much more quickly and less expensively than by pen plotting. Complex graphic screen displays may be copied by the touch of a button. This includes any combination of graphic and nongraphic (text) display. The entire process requires but a few seconds. The copy, however, does not approach the level of quality produced by the pen plotter. Thus, it is used primarily for preliminary check prints rather than final copy. It is, for example, very useful for a quick preview at various intermediate steps of a design project.

Popular hard copy devices include the electrostatic method, the ink jet process, and the photo plotter. These are considered raster devices since the output is in a dot matrix form.

- *Electrostatic method.* The electrostatic method is the most popular. It uses a fine array of nibs to electrically charge small dots on the medium. The image is then permanently placed on the charged surface with toner. A vector-to-raster conversion process has hampered effectiveness and increased expense.
- *Ink jet process.* The ink jet process deposits various colored-ink droplets on the medium. As with the electrostatic method, expense and conversion have been the barriers to overcome.
- *Photo plotter.* A typical photo plotter is shown in Fig. 2-25. One process involves the use of fiber-optics technology to produce the image on dry silver paper. The unit shown produces a small A size copy that is satisfactory for quick preview during intermediate work steps.

Other less popular types of hard copy units are available. Some are the dot matrix impact and the thermoprinter.

Fig. 2-25 Hard copy unit.

Courtesy Tektronix, Inc.

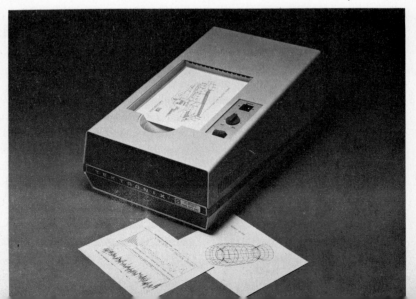

2-13 Computer-Aided Manufacturing: Numerical Control

Computer-aided manufacturing (CAM) uses the result of a computer-aided design. Combining CAD and CAM has had the effect of radically increasing productivity and accuracy. When CAD is used to prepare the design of a product, the instructions for the manufacture or preparation of that design are sent directly to the factory. One method of transmitting the information is known as *numerical control* (NC). Numerical control tapes and equipment can store the designs that are used with a variety of production-related processes without producing an actual engineering drawing. In other words, the information is transmitted directly from one data base to another data base. The NC tape is actually the drawing on a different medium.

CAM accomplishes process planning and processing among other tasks. Process planning is the sequence of production steps. Mechanical processing has to do with tool-path creation. Tool-path movement is controlled by an NC tape. Output of the CRT is punched onto a tape. The tape is not the same as the cassette tapes previously described. It is prepared by the selective placement of holes in paper, such as that shown in Fig. 2-26. The punched tape converts the image on the screen to recorded coded information.

Fig. 2-26 Numerical control tape.

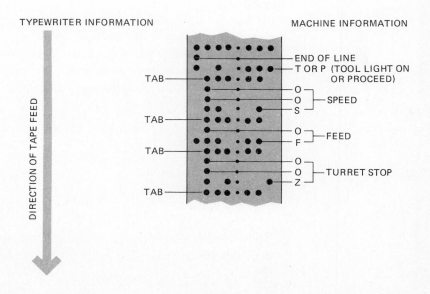

This information describes each desired movement of the machine. Thus, NC machining is computer-controlled machining. A machine operator is not required. The punched tape is an output of the CRT. The finished (manufactured) part is an output of the tape. Note that NC eliminates the need for a hard-copy engineering drawing. The drawing is stored in a data base known as a *geometrical data base*.

Modern NC equipment allows three-axis (X-Y-Z) generation, or movement: forward-backward, left-right, and up-down. The machines that are controlled are the common types found in industry—lathes, drilling machines, and milling machines, for example.

2-14 Computer-Aided Manufacturing: Robotics

The newest feature of computer-aided manufacturing is known as *robotics*. Robot machinery appears similar to the CRT display shown in Fig. 2-27. It differs from NC machinery in that movement is now the prime duty. Automatic manipulators are used to perform a variety of materials-handling functions. The robot manipulators are arms and hands. They will grasp, operate, assemble, and handle. Robot manipulators are especially useful in environments intolerable to human beings. They may be delicate enough to pick up an egg, yet strong enough to exert a great force on large steel products.

As stated earlier, NC equipment has three-axis movement. Robots have the ability to move about in the X, Y, and Z directions. This includes six degrees of freedom. A degree of freedom is constrained or unconstrained movement. For example, the ability to turn or rotate. On a robot these are known as:

- Waist.
- Shoulder.
- Elbow.
- Wrist rotation.
- Wrist bending.
- Flange.

These modes allow essentially any positioning. A simplistic version of this control is similar to the two-axis (X-Y) pen plotter out-

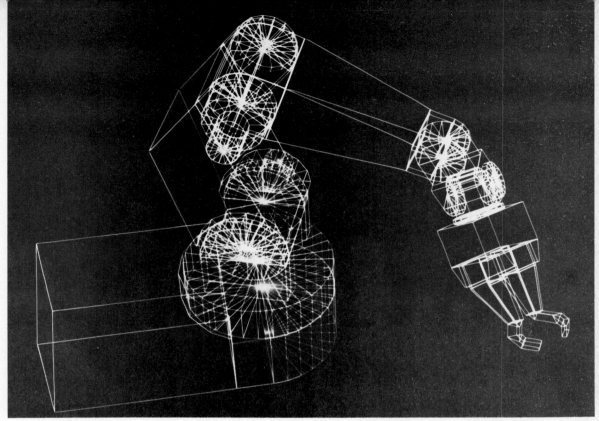

Fig. 2-27 Robot display on a CRT.

put. Robots also may be controlled by a digitizer or a light pen. An instruction is sent to the arm.

The ultimate aim of many in industry is to organize *every* step of manufacturing around computer automation. This is happening in some countries, such as Japan, where certain industries are controlled by personnel in the engineering and design office who have the ability to both create and produce products. Robotics provides the potential for the "totally automated industrial facility."

Summary

This chapter dealt with a description of CAD system equipment. In addition, concepts such as computer-aided manufacturing (CAM) were introduced. Every major type of equipment was covered in detail. The intent, however, was to focus on the equipment most likely to be encountered. Some overlap is seen to exist in determining if the equipment is considered as part of input, output, or processing. For example, the alphanumeric keyboard actually controls input. It is almost always, however, a part of a package with the CRT—a combination commonly referred to as a terminal.

Several devices are used to control the CRT cursor position. They may be called processing controls since they are used to control steps in the drawing process. The devices include:

- *Stylus or puck*. The stylus or puck is positioned on a graphics tablet. An electronic grid network under the tablet surface senses the location of the coordinates. This location is transmitted to the screen via the CPU.
- *Joystick*. The joystick is pushed in a direction, and the cursor is correspondingly repositioned in the same direction.
- *Thumbwheel*. Thumbwheels are normally located directly on the terminal. One controls a horizontal line; the other, a vertical line. The intersection of these lines locates the cursor position.
- *Light pen*. The light pen is activated directly on the screen. It is pointed to the desired position.

None of the control devices is considered superior to any other. Each type works well. A person's preference depends primarily upon how the person was trained.

Systems are combined with various pieces of the equipment described. The combination depends on the needs and financial status of the company. The very large main frame CAD systems have had costs exceeding 1 million dollars. The small micro and mini CAD systems, having more limited capability, cost only a small fraction of that figure. No matter which type of equipment is used, manufacturers attempt to continually simplify system operation—to make systems more *user friendly*. Users are not required to know programming techniques. They can rely on a large availability of programs, or software.

The state of the art in CAD is still evolving. Future systems will be likely to include such features as a device enabling the user to "talk" to the computer. The ultimate goal of CAD includes a full implementation with CAM for a totally automated factory.

Terms to Know

Alphanumeric keyboard A keyboard similar to the typewriter keyboard. Allows the user to input letter (alpha) and number (numeric) instructions to the central processor.

Binary	The base 2 numbering system. Uses only the digits 0 and 1.
Bit	Taken from *b*inary dig*it*. It is a 0 or 1 signal.
Byte	A sequence of binary digits (bits) that the computer operates on as a single unit. It is eight bits and is the basis of comparison used in describing various systems and manufacturers. One byte is a character of memory. A megabyte would be 1 million characters.
Character	A coded symbol for a digit or letter. Actually the same as a byte.
Computer	Popular name referring to the CPU. It additionally includes the graphic display station and alphanumeric keyboard on small systems.
CPU	Central processing unit. The microprocessor portion of the computer that accomplishes the logical processing of data. The CPU contains the arithmetic, logic, and control circuits, and possibly the memory storage.
Cursor	The bright mark on the CRT that moves and locates positions on the screen. May be variously shaped (dot, cross hair, check, and so on).
Dedicated	Used with a single terminal by one user. Said of a microprocessor generally used for one type of work. A dedicated system stands alone and does not hook in to any larger computer to complete work.
Desk-top computer	A dedicated computer small enough to be located on the user's desk.
Digitizer	A term commonly used to describe a graphics tablet.
Digitizing	The method by which data is entered on a graphics tablet. A stylus or puck is "touched down" at a particular location. This touching down is called digitizing.
Floppy disk	A thin, flexible (nonrigid) disk that stores programs.
Function board	A keyboard that allows for graphic data entry of various functions; for example, pressing a LINE program button will allow the input of a line onto the CRT.

Graphic display station	The unit that displays the image or drawing. The most popular graphic display stations are CRTs.
Graphics tablet	An input device having a flat surface on which the work is done. A stylus or a puck is used for the graphical data entry. Information is transmitted to the CRT by means of an electrically controlled grid beneath the tablet's surface.
Hard copy	A preliminary drawing that is produced by the hard copy unit and is often used as a checkprint.
Host	One central place where the data resides.
Joystick	An input device which directly controls the cursor. The stick is moved in the same direction as the user wishes the cursor to move on the screen.
Light pen	An input pointing device. Data entry may be made directly onto the screen by positioning and activating the tip of the pen at the desired location.
Mainframe	A CPU utilized with many terminals for multipurpose use.
Mask	An interchangeable sheet often made of plastic. It fits over a function board, menu pad, or graphics tablet.
Memory	Stored information, programs, and data inside automated equipment. One byte is a character of memory.
Menu	A selection from which the designer or drafter can choose various functions.
Menu pad	Also known as a menu tablet. An input device having a flat surface on which functions are selected using a stylus or puck. Similar to a function board without buttons.
Micro	The smallest type of CAD system. Micros are dedicated units using home computers.
Mini	A CAD system having capabilities between a micro and a mainframe. Minis are generally dedicated for the specific purpose of the user. This type of CAD system is commonly used in industry.
NC	Numerical control. The use of computer-generated instructions to manufacture a part.
Peripheral	Additional equipment working in conjunction with, but not as part of, the computer.

Plotter	An output device. A drawing of the screen display is automatically generated onto a plotter.
RAM	Random access memory. Temporary memory: information can be written in or read out and lost when power is turned off.
Raster	A network or matrix of dots. Each dot falls within a square area known as a pixel.
Refresh	The method of redrawing each line of a graphic display.
Resolution	The number of addressable dots per unit area. Low-resolution screens produce jogged lines.
ROM	Read-only memory. Permanent memory: information is stored permanently and is read out.
Robot	A system that simulates human activities from computer instruction.
Stand-alone	Similar to *dedicated*.
Terminal	Popular name given to the combination of a visual display screen (CRT) and keyboard.
Vector	Producing straight lines between two points.
Voice-activated	Systems that can recognize and respond to spoken words.

Questions

1. Why is a CAD application referred to as interactive?
2. What is the most popular type of graphics display station?
3. What is the primary use of the alphanumeric keyboard?
4. What are the three types of CAD systems?
5. Which system accounts for the majority of early systems?
6. What are two common CAD programming languages?
7. What is the most popular means of storing programs for use with minisystems?
8. Why is a graphics tablet called a *digitizer?*
9. What does reference to the term *cursor* mean?
10. What are the major devices used to control a cursor?
11. Which cursor control device is the best to use?
12. What are pen plotters primarily used for?
13. What are the popular types of pen plotters?
14. What are the popular types of hard copy units?
15. What is the result of combining CAD with the numerical control part of CAM?
16. What is the ultimate goal of CAD/CAM?

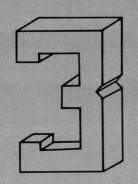

Shape and Size Description or Generation

3-1 Basic Commands and Functions

This chapter will cover the procedures required to produce a *basic* engineering drawing using CAD. Each procedure will be referred to as a command or function. A *command* is a series of directions used to execute a function. A *function* is the producing of a change in the display on a CRT screen. For example, the addition of a line to a displayed drawing is a function. The directions used to implement the function constitute a command. The term *command,* however, is common among drafters and is often used to describe any action. The steps for each procedure will be treated in a general manner and as broadly as possible. This way, each may be applied to a variety of applications and equipment. The result of a function or command is universal. The procedure, however, varies somewhat from system to system. Thus, case studies showing a certain specific method of a particular system will be used.

In general, the basic functions, commands, or objects of commands are similar. This text will categorize them as:

- Geometry generators.
- Size generators.
- Geometry modifiers.

The geometry generators are those particular functions that enable a graphical shape to be described on the CRT. These are:

- Point.
- Line.
- Circle, ellipse, or arc.
- Irregular curve or spline.

55

After the shape of an object is complete, its size must be described. This nongraphical work may be accomplished by size generators. In design and drafting, these functions are known as:

- Dimensioning.
- Text (notes).

The geometry generators supply the geometric shapes basic to any system. Geometry modifiers are used to finish off or complete the shape description. These commands may vary between systems but generally include such items as:

- Type.
- Dragging (relimit).
- Corner.

The proper combining and execution of each generator and modifier listed enables an individual to prepare an engineering drawing. Even though each function is basic to an engineering drawing, the method of combining will vary. It will depend on system capability (micro, mini, or mainframe) and the type of input equipment available. Several methods are available to execute procedures. The equipment used will vary and may include:

- Keyboard X-Y coordinate input.
- Function board.
- Light pen.
- Digitizer (graphics tablet).
- Joystick.
- Other specialized methods.

It is common to use one piece of equipment in conjunction with another. For example, a light pen or digitizer may be used to locate a position. A function board then can be used to transmit a message. The result is displayed on the CRT screen.

The CAD system helps guide you through the various aspects of drawing development. Written instruction appears on the CRT screen to accomplish this. The instructions, referred to as *prompts, cues, message options,* or *message lines,* may appear in any location on the screen. Some systems utilize a dual-screen setup. One screen is for the graphics; the other is for prompting the user. An example of this is shown in Fig. 2-3(c). In either case, prompting makes CAD easier to use.

The following sections in this chapter will demonstrate the use of methods and combinations of methods for basic execution. First, however, the system must be turned on by a start-up procedure.

3-2 Start-up

Before any graphical data can be displayed on the CRT screen, the system must be turned on. Each CAD manufacturer has a start-up procedure. For micro and mini systems, this may include checking that each piece of equipment is plugged in (connected) to a convenience outlet (duplex wall receptacle). If the system is new to the user, total power consumption of the system should be determined. In a large company, you may not need to know this. In a small office, however, it may be your responsibility to ensure that power capability is not exceeded.

Power consumption can be found in the manufacturer's user manual or on a nameplate. A nameplate is attached to each piece of equipment. Total all of the individual power requirements. In general, the total should not exceed 80 percent of the convenience branch circuit rating. Often, a no. 12 American wire gage with a 20-ampere (20-A) protective device is used for 120-volt (120-V) receptacle circuits. If this is the case, the total power requirements of the CAD system should be 16 A or less. Should the ratings by the manufacturer be given in watts (W), divide the total by 120 (for 120-V systems) to estimate the current draw (in amperes). The total may exceed the capability of one circuit. Connect the excess equipment to a duplex receptacle on a different branch circuit. The smaller the system, the less likelihood of an electrical problem.

After the pieces of equipment have been connected to the power supply, the system may be turned on. A typical procedure for mini system is given here.

1. First, turn on any peripherals (graphics tablet, plotter, etc.) by pushing the power switches. Power switches may be located on the front of, beneath, at either side of, or at the rear of the equipment. An example of this is shown in Fig. 3-1. This particular switch is located on the rear panel of a graphics tablet console.

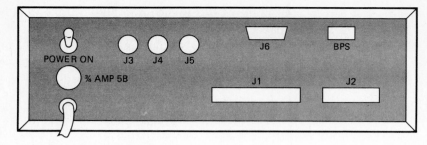

Fig. 3-1 Power switch.

2. After a brief warm-up period (several seconds to be safe), the terminal may be switched on in a like manner.

3. Insert the appropriate software if it is not already in place.

4. A small system may use a tape or disk with several stored programs. In this case, you will want to display a listing of the contents. This is accomplished differently with different manufacturers. A common method is to press a button or key to call up the contents. One manufacturer calls this button *Auto-load*. If a tape is used, you may first have to rewind it by pressing a Rewind button.

5. The contents of the software is now displayed on the screen. The user may act accordingly by selecting the appropriate program or function. A program may be selected by the alphanumeric keyboard on the terminal. Larger mini systems, such as the one illustrated in Fig. 2-20, provide for alphanumeric input directly from a graphics tablet menu. For such systems, either the menu or keyboard may be used. Examples in this chapter will be confined to keyboard input.

6. A function may now be selected by a program board. The execution methods will be discussed later in detail. Note: a sophisticated mini system may not require Steps 3 through 6. The software will be immediately initiated after Step 2.

7. You may break communication with the computer at any time by turning off the terminal power switch. Caution: when the main power supply is broken, all work accomplished since the last file may be lost. A *file* is a recording of the work developed during that session. As a user

develops a drawing, he or she may periodically store the drawing. The work accomplished will then not be lost. Work is stored by either manual or automatic filing, depending on the system.

Mainframe systems will have the software initially intact. These systems may be started by *logging on*. This may entail simply selecting start by using an on/off button. More likely, however, alphanumeric keyboard, or light pen input will also be needed. An example of a sign-on procedure includes the following.

1. Key in a code number (e.g., CAD 0019). This number will correspond to your identification number.
2. Select a FILE program button on the function board. This is typical of most systems. A numeric list of available files or drawings will be displayed on the screen (e.g., 001, 002, 003).
3. A stored drawing in the file may be selected by use of a light pen (e.g., press pen to drawing 001).
4. A new drawing may be started by keying in the number that is one higher than those listed on the file.

Remember, each manufacturer has its own start-up procedure. Also, it should be noted that logging on is accomplished with the aid of prompts. The system will display the instructions or prompts. The above examples are typical; however, consult the specific manufacturer user's manual for exact instructions.

3-3 Point

After the system has been started, data may be entered. Be sure the correct program or menu is used (if required). Data entry may be graphical or nongraphical. The most basic entry of data is the location and display of a point on the CRT screen. As previously mentioned, this may be accomplished in many ways. The common ones will be described.

Alphanumeric Input

Use an alphanumeric keyboard, similar to the one shown in Fig. 2-5. Key in the desired point location by following this procedure.

1. Press the key or keys describing the desired X (horizontal) value: e.g., −3. Without the aid of software, a system will require you to type the word MOVE first.
2. If each coordinate must be input separately, press an End or Return key as shown in Fig. 2-5. If the coordinates are to be input collectively, enter a comma.
3. Press the key or keys describing the desired Y (vertical) value: e.g., −2.5.
4. Press End or Return. This is the same step as the carriage return on a typewriter. A point will appear at the desired coordinate location: e.g., −3, −2.5. The cursor display may be a bright or blinking mark, dot, element, cross hair, etc. Figure 3-2(a) shows the desired point (dark cross hair) located with respect to coordinates 0, 0 which are located at the center of the screen (light cross hair). Other systems may locate the zero coordinates at the lower left corner. In either case, any number of points may be positioned on the screen. Follow the procedure of Steps 1 through 4 for each additional point. For example, a second point located at X = 2.5 and Y = 2 is shown in Fig. 3-2(b) by the dark cross hair.

This method, while very accurate, is not used often. It is somewhat cumbersome, and CAD software packages have quicker entry means. Most CAD techniques attempt to make daily work more and more like traditional drafting. Thus, the keyboard is used primarily for nongraphic work.

Fig. 3-2 Point positioning.

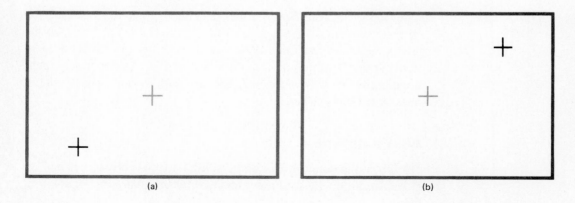

(a)   (b)

Function Board

A function board, function keyboard, or menu pad, may be used to enter a point. It offers quicker point entry than the separate keying in of each coordinate. An appropriate program is connected to the buttons on the board. Each allows a particular function to occur. One method of accomplishing point generation is through the use of a joystick.

1. Use the joystick to position the cursor at the desired location of the point. This is accomplished by the method described in Sec. 2-10.
2. Press a POINT program button on a function board. The point will be located as shown in Fig. 3.2.

The drawback to this method is that point placement is not accurate. The point appears only in the general vicinity desired since a joystick is difficult to control. This drawback can be partially corrected by the use of a grid pattern on the screen. An example of a grid pattern is shown in Fig. 3-3. Grid points are located equidistant from each other. A point will be positioned at the nearest grid point. To accomplish this, use the joystick to move the cursor. When the cursor appears near a desired point, press the POINT program button. The point is located. This location is determined by the size of the grid pattern. The problem with a grid pattern is that points cannot be located between grids. The program used to display the grid pattern would have to be changed by the computer programmer. Distance between the grid points would be de-

Fig. 3-3 Grid pattern on screen.

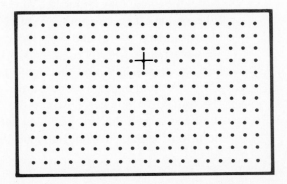

creased. The change would result in a new grid pattern. Again, however, locations occur only in relation to points on the modified pattern.

Digitizing

Two common methods are used to place a point on the screen by means of a graphics tablet. One is by use of a menu located either on the tablet surface or on an accompanying tablet or board. The other is with the aid of a function board. In either case, software containing a POINT program must be used. Also, the graphics tablet must be activated. The console, as shown in Fig. 2-19, is set in the POINT mode. With some equipment it can be started simply by supplying power as descibed in Sec. 3-2. With others, the origin (lower left) and the rectangular area or the size (four corners) must be located. A stylus or puck is used for this purpose. The use of the stylus involves depressing the point of it (or touching down) at a desired location. If a puck is used, some means such as cross hairs must be provided. These will define the touch-down location on the graphics tablet or graphics tablet menu. Thus, to set the area or size, depress the stylus or puck at each of four corners. These define the corners of an imaginary rectangle and, thus, determine the surface area of the drawing.

If the graphics tablet has the means to accommodate a menu offering, a stylus will place a point on the screen.

1. Depress a stylus (shown in Fig. 2-18) on the main area of the tablet at the desired location. The network beneath senses this location.
2. Using a stylus or puck, select POINT from a menu. Note: the menu may be located directly on the tablet surface or on a separate unit. Typical menu displays are shown in Fig. 3-4(a) and (b). Depress the stylus within the area marked POINT. A network beneath the tablet surface senses this, and the signal is transmitted to the CRT. A point appears on the screen in relation to where the stylus first touched down on the tablet. If the stylus digitized a position on the lower left of the tablet, the point on the screen would also be located on the lower left.

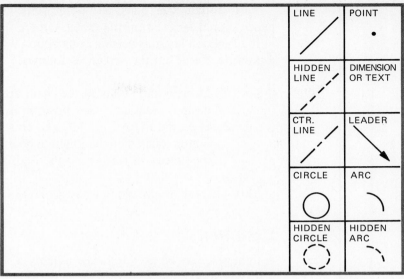

(a)

	MAIN AREA OF TABLET _(USED FOR DRAWING CREATION)_				
DIGITIZER WINDOW	**INPUT PARAMETERS**			**DIGITIZER MODE**	**KEYBOARD**
RECTANGULAR	LINE TYPE	TEXT HEIGHT	TEXT FONT	LINE	
MULTIPOINT	SET ROUNDNESS			RECTANGLE	
	GRID ROUNDOFF			CIRCLE	
				ARC CW	
				ARC CCW	
				TEXT	
				STREAM	

(b)

Fig. 3-4(a) Menu display on graphics tablet. (b) Partial menu display on graphics tablet.

This method can place the point somewhat accurately. Grid paper should be used on the tablet surface for accuracy.

If a function board is used in conjunction with the graphics tablet, a point is placed on the screen as follows.

1. Depress the stylus in the main area of the tablet at the desired location. This position is sensed by the tablet.
2. Press the POINT (or MOVE, on some boards,) program button located on the function board. A point appears on the screen in relation to the digitized position.

This method is also somewhat accurate if grid paper is used.

Light Pen

A light pen may be used to locate a point in several different ways. It may be used either with or without the aid of a function board. To locate a point with the function board, do the following.

1. Use the pen to point to the desired location on the screen.
2. Next, activate the pen by pressing it against the screen.
3. Press the appropriate button on the function board. A point appears at the location.

This method is very easy to use; however, the accuracy is only as close as the user can visually estimate.

A second method that works well is when the two lines that intersect are shown on the screen. The point of intersection between them can easily be determined.

1. Select one of the lines and activate the pen.
2. Select the other line and activate the pen.
3. Press the appropriate button on the function board.

The point appears at the intersection of the lines. This method is not only easy to perform but is also very accurate.

Several other methods may be used to generate a point. Some manufacturers display instructions and menu directly on the screen. Other manufacturers use two screens: One is for drawing preparation; the other displays written instructions or prompts. The instructions, or menu selection, may be produced by a button on the function board. A stylus or puck on a menu pad may also be used. In either case, the display will appear on a screen.

One example of instructions displayed on a screen is shown in Fig. 3-5. The display may be in either a horizontal or a vertical format. The menu of available operations in Fig. 3-5 is shown across the bottom of the screen. Selecting POINT with the light pen will display the word POINT at the upper left of the screen, indicating that points may now be input. The upper right of the screen shows the instructions the user follows in order to cause a specific point to be displayed. These instructions, also referred to as message options, prompts, or message lines, are arranged in order of priority and may be displayed in either a horizontal or vertical format. In the example in Fig. 3-5, first attention is given to KEY X. This instruction means that the alphanumeric method may be used and that the X coordinate should be keyed in first. When this is done, the Y coordinate is next keyed in. Next, attention is given to the IND PT (indicate point) option. This means that the user may press the appropriate button on the function board to indicate a point if desired. The last attention is given to the instruction SEL ANY. This means any point may be selected using the light pen. The user can use any of the above options.

Manufacturers offer a wide variety of menu selections. Each method is unique to the manufacturer's equipment. Space does not permit covering each in detail. The one method shown above is to serve only as an example. It will give you some familiarity with the way a large system operates. Note the large variety of options that are available in the placement of a point on the screen.

Fig. 3-5 Display screen (from POINT program).

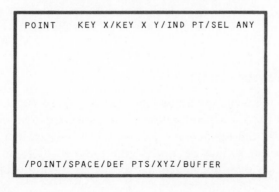

```
POINT    KEY X/KEY X Y/IND PT/SEL ANY




















/POINT/SPACE/DEF PTS/XYZ/BUFFER
```

3-4
Line

Placing a line on the screen of the CRT is an extension of the point procedure. In general, if two points (or positions) have been found, they determine the endpoints of a line. Depending on the position of the second point relative to the first, a line may be drawn horizontally, vertically, or at any angle. The common methods to accomplish the placement of a line on the CRT follow.

Alphanumeric Input

The keyboard on a terminal can be used to input instructions to generate a line. A short program must be composed. It would consist of locating a point, moving the cursor to a second point location, then performing the draw operation. A sample program used to draw three lines is shown in Fig. 1-3. Since software is always available, however, it is not necessary to create a program each time one wishes to draw a line. A more likely method of creating a line using the keyboard follows.

1. Key in the desired X and Y values for the first endpoint: e.g., 2.5, 2.5.
2. Press the End or Return key. The first endpoint will be displayed as shown in Fig. 3-6(a).
3. Key in the desired X and Y values for the second endpoint: e.g., 4.5, 2.5. It will be located as indicated in Fig. 3-6(b).
4. Press the appropriate key and/or program button. The line will appear on the screen at the desired location as shown in Fig. 3-6(c). It begins 2.5 units up and 2.5 units over to the right (positive direction) from the origin. It will be horizontal and 2.0 units long. Note: this display is relative to an origin located at the screen center. This method, while time consuming, is absolute (exact).

Function Board

Line generation may be executed using a function board containing a LINE program button. The method also involves positioning and moving the cursor on the screen. Various input devices, such as a joystick, may be used to move and position the cursor. The cursor also may be moved and positioned using a function board only.

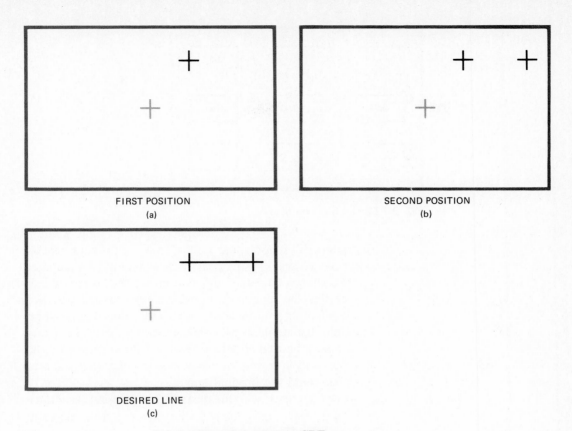

FIRST POSITION
(a)

SECOND POSITION
(b)

DESIRED LINE
(c)

Fig. 3-6 Line placement on CRT.

This is done with program buttons similar to those shown in Fig. 3-7.

The method of drawing a line using a function board is as follows.

1. The initial position of the cursor is normally at the origin, as shown in Fig. 3-8(a). If this is not the desired position of the first endpoint, it can be moved. Use any or all of the four direction buttons on the function board. These are illustrated in Fig. 3-7 by arrows that show the direction of movement. For example, to move the cursor vertically up, push the button ↑. To move up and over to the right, push buttons ↑ and →, and so on. The distance moved at each press of the button has been prepro-

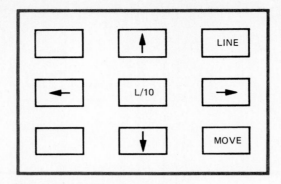

Fig. 3-7 Partial function board.

grammed. If too great or too small a distance results from each press, it may easily be changed. A computer programmer can alter the portion of the program that specifies the length by removing the original distance specification and inserting a different one. A program button that automatically changes the *step* (distance) may also be found on certain systems. One is shown by the center button in Fig. 3-7: pressing it will reduce the step to one-tenth the original length.

2. After the cursor is in the desired first position, as shown in Fig. 3-8(b), push the MOVE program button shown in Fig. 3-7. This allows movement to, and positioning of, the cursor at the new location and makes the first point appear on the screen. This important function will be further emphasized in Chap. 4, where it is used to prepare a multiview drawing.

3. Position the second endpoint as described in Step 1. The screen will now appear as seen in Fig. 3-8(c).

4. Press the LINE program button of Fig. 3-7. The desired line appears on the screen as shown in Figure 3-8(d).

5. Additional lines may be drawn by repeating Steps 3 and 4. Each new line will be attached to the last line endpoint unless the MOVE program button is used. Note: the MOVE program button allows you to reposition the cursor location without drawing a line.

You should now be able to prepare the outline of an object having any number of horizontal, vertical, or inclined lines. Each line

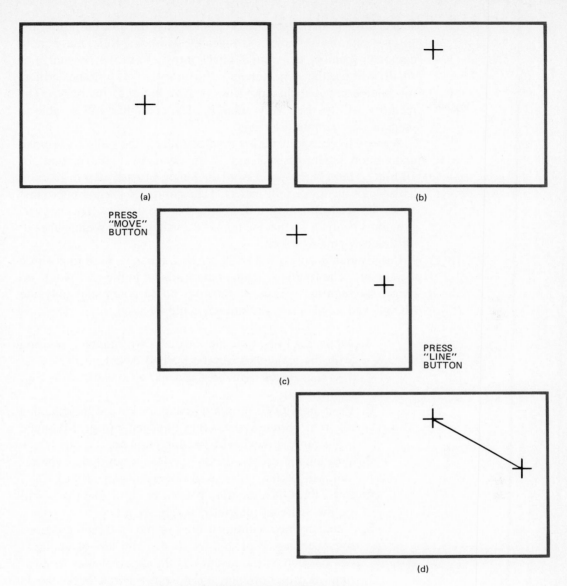

PRESS "MOVE" BUTTON

PRESS "LINE" BUTTON

(a)

(b)

(c)

(d)

Fig. 3-8 Drawing a line on the screen.

represents an object line on a drawing. One drawback to this method is that it is only as accurate as the length of the moves. These steps, of course, can be changed to become very small increments (e.g., 0.05 in). The problem then becomes the time it takes to position the second endpoint of a long line. For example, if each step is 0.05 in, to draw a 5-in horizontal line, the user must push the → or ← button 100 times. Besides the additional time, much more computer memory is required. Each move, no matter how large or small, will use the same amount of memory. This becomes critical for microcomputers having 16K or 32K bytes of memory. The memory will be used very quickly. The computer will be able to prepare only simple drawings.

A more likely application would be to have the steps correspond to common increments such as 0.25 in (decimal), ¼ in (fraction), or 10 mm. Note: in the processor, the length of each step is given in units—not inches or millimeters. The computer programmer must check the real and apparent dimensions of the device. This conversion must be made so that the numerical values are in scale inches or millimeters on the screen.

If a joystick is connected to the system, it can be used to position the cursor. The four positioning button shown in Fig. 3-7 would no longer be required. Thus, a function board containing only the MOVE and LINE program buttons could be used.

1. Move the cursor to the desired first endpoint position with the joystick using the method described in Sec. 2-10. The result will be the same as illustrated in Fig. 3-8(b).
2. Push the MOVE program button, or key, to indicate this position. Some systems may use a letter (e.g., M) on the alphanumeric keyboard for this purpose.
3. Position the second endpoint with the joystick. The result will be the same as illustrated in Fig. 3-8(c).
4. Press the LINE program button, or key. The result will be the same as illustrated in Fig. 3-8(d).
5. You can draw additional lines or move to new positions by repeating Steps 1 through 4. The use of an input device such as the joystick is the quickest way to position. Again, however, it is only as accurate as the user's hand and eye. The use of a grid pattern system as described in Sec. 3-3, under "Function Board," and illustrated in Fig. 3-3 will improve this situation.

Digitizing

As described in Sec. 3-3, under "Digitizing," there are two common methods using a graphics tablet. A line may be placed on the screen either by use of a menu or with the aid of the function board. The procedure using a stylus with a menu similar to that of Fig. 3-4(a) is given here.

1. Use a stylus similar to one shown in Fig. 2-18. Depress the stylus on the main area of the tablet at the first desired location. The network beneath the tablet surface senses the location of the first endpoint.
2. Again depress the stylus at the desired second endpoint. This location is also sensed by the tablet.
3. Next, select a LINE program from a menu as shown in Fig. 3-4(a). Depress the stylus anywhere within the area so marked. The signal is transmitted to the CRT, and a line appears on the screen. The location and accuracy is similar to that described in Sec. 3-3, under "Digitizing." A series of continuous lines can be placed very rapidly on the screen by the repetition of Steps 2 and 3.

Hidden (or dashed) lines and center lines may be drawn in a similar fashion. Simply select the appropriate menu from Fig. 3-4(a) using a stylus.

An actual case study of line generation is presented in Appendix I. A specific manufacturer, in this case Tektronix, Inc., is used for the illustration. It provides an excellent example of an actual industrial method.

If a function board is used in conjunction with a graphics tablet, the procedure becomes the following.

1. Locate and depress the stylus at one endpoint of the desired line. This position is sensed by the tablet.
2. Press the MOVE program button. One manufacturer uses the word INDICATE; still others may use a different word. A point appears on the screen in relation to where the stylus digitized. It will appear similar to that shown in Fig. 3-8(b).
3. Depress the stylus at the second endpoint. This position is sensed by the tablet and appears on the screen as shown in Fig. 3-8(c).
4. Press the LINE program button. A line will appear on the screen similar to that shown in Fig. 3-8(d). Successive lines may rapidly be drawn on the screen by repeating Steps 3 and 4.

Light Pen

As described in Sec. 3-3 under "Light Pen," the light pen may be used several ways. A common method utilizes a function board and menu display. A typical procedure consists of the following steps.

1. Depress the LINE program button on a function board. A menu is displayed on the screen. One such illustration is shown in Fig. 3-9.
2. Any type of line may be selected from the menu shown across the bottom of the display. For example, if a horizontal line is desired, select HORIZ by pressing the light pen against it.
3. If one endpoint exists, select it with the light pen. This point may become one end of a horizontal line. An endpoint can be displayed by the method described in Sec. 3-3, under "Light Pen."
4. Instructions are listed across the upper right of the screen. They indicate the ways a line can be put on the screen. First, attention is given to the alphanumeric keyboard. On the alphanumeric, key in the desired length (e.g., −2.0) and press the End or Return button.
5. Determine the horizontal direction (left or right) by placing the light pen to the side desired. Activate the appropriate switch or button. The line is displayed.

Another case study of line generation is shown in Appendix II. This method is presented with the IBM, Lockheed, and Adage com-

Fig. 3-9 Line menu and prompt display on CRT.

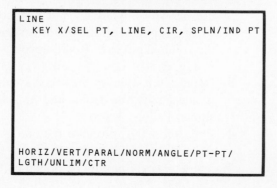

```
LINE
   KEY X/SEL PT, LINE, CIR, SPLN/IND PT




HORIZ/VERT/PARAL/NORM/ANGLE/PT-PT/
LGTH/UNLIM/CTR
```

bined system. The system is known as CADAM. (CADAM is a registered trademark of CADAM Inc.) It utilizes a light pen. Note the difference between this method and the example in Appendix I.

A line can easily be displayed if both endpoints are known. One procedure that accomplishes this is the following.

1. Select PT-PT (point-to-point) from the menu selection in Fig. 3-9 using the light pen. The instructions at the upper right change to KEY X, Y/SEL ELEM/IND PT.
2. Select the first desired endpoint—SEL ELEM (select element), the second instruction option—using the light pen.
3. Select the second desired endpoint using the light pen. The desired line will appear after activating the light pen. It may be horizontal, vertical, or at any angle.

A line of unlimited length can be drawn as follows.

1. Select UNLIM (unlimited) from the menu in Fig. 3-9 using the light pen. The instructions change to KEY Y/SEL PT, LINE, CIR/IND PT
2. If any point on the line is known, select it (SEL PT) with the light pen. A line (horizontal, if you have selected a HORIZONTAL mode) of unlimited length will be drawn. If a point is not available, key in the coordinate, or the Y value. A horizontal line of unlimited length will be drawn at that coordinate.

For an unlimited vertical line, select VERT from the menu in Fig. 3-9. Repeat Steps 1 and 2 keying in the desired X value.

Another method using both a light pen and a menu board consists of the following.

1. A text menu similar to the partial listing below is used. The text is abbreviated. For example, INS means *insert*, ERS means *erase*, and PNT means *point*.

VERBS	NOUNS	MODIFIERS		PUNC
INS	LTR	PRL	PRP	:
ERS	CTR	HOR	VERT	;
MOVE	PNT	ON	OFF	,
ROT	ARC	ALL	EXC	.
MIR	LIN			

2. To draw a line, first select the INS (insert) program with the light pen.
3. Next, select the LIN (line) program with the light pen.
4. Next, select the : (colon) program with the light pen. The colon is used to signal the end of the direction.
5. A line is generated when you use the light pen to select two positions on the screen.

Many different procedures are used to draw lines using the light pen. They vary with the manufacturer. The ones explained in this section illustrate typical examples.

3-5 Circle

Circle construction includes ellipses, arcs, or parts of circles. In addition, the lines may be solid or dashed. These may be used to describe various types of lines (object, hidden, or center) as may be required on an engineering drawing. There are several ways to accomplish each procedure, depending on the software. Different programs will require different input data. Common input variables include:

- Center point and radius.
- Edge, or tangent, point and radius.
- Two points and radius.
- Three points.
- Center point and major and minor axes.
- Center point, radius, start angle, and end angle.

Procedures will be developed that include one, several, or combinations of the above variables.

Alphanumeric Input

To produce a circle by the keyboard without the aid of a program is not feasible. The procedure would consist of drawing many short straight lines simulating the circle. The shorter each line, or step, the more the completed figure would appear as a circle. Thus, to draw a circle using 10° steps for each line would require 36 operations similar to that described in Sec. 3-4, under "Alphanumeric Input." A program to draw a circle having 120° steps would be similar to the one in Fig. 1-3(a). This, of course, consists of three steps which form a triangle as shown in Fig. 1-3(b). The most common way to generate a circle with alphanumeric input is in response to a function program button.

Function Board and Alphanumeric Input

The general method to produce a circle follows.

1. Select the CIRCLE program button on the function board. A set of instructions will appear on the screen. One such display appears in Fig. 3-10(a).
2. Using the first instruction option, use the keyboard to input the desired X value (e.g., 2.75) and press the End or Return button.
3. Next, key in the desired Y value (e.g., 2.75) and press the End or Return button. The CRT may display the origin of the circle as shown in Fig. 3-10(b).
4. Key in the desired radius (e.g., 1.0) and press the End or Return button. A circle will be displayed as shown in Fig. 3-10(c). Its location will be 2.75 up and 2.75 over from the origin, and it will have a diameter of 2.0. Units (i.e., inches, millimeters, etc.) will depend on the program setup.

A set of instructions similar to that shown in Fig. 3-11(a) might also be used. The instructions are more extensive and will require more time. They are more general in nature, however, and can be expanded to produce either a circle, an ellipse, or an arc. The procedure involves following the displayed instructions.

1. Locate the desired center of the circle by a cursor movement. Use function keys or an input device such as a joystick.
2. Press the CIRCLE or ELLIPSE program button. Instructions will be displayed on the screen. The program may give the option of drawing the circle from its edge (circumference) or from its center.
3. If the cursor is in the center of the circle, rather than at the edge of it, key in Yes (Y on the keyboard) or Center (C on the keyboard) response. Press End or Return.

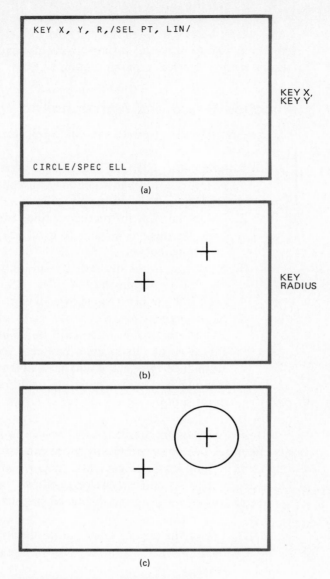

```
KEY X, Y, R,/SEL PT, LIN/



                                              KEY X,
                                              KEY Y




CIRCLE/SPEC ELL
```
(a)

KEY
RADIUS

(b)

(c)

Fig. 3-10 Placing a circle on CRT.

The response depends on how the program has been set up.
4. Next key in the number of degrees for the graphic display.
   a. If a full circle or ellipse is desired, key in:

- 0 (starting point in degrees)
- End or Return
- 360 (ending point in degrees)
- End or Return

b. If a 90° arc is desired, key in:
- 0 (starting point in degrees)
- End or Return
- 90 (ending point in degrees)
- End or Return

The instructions will shape a 90° arc in the position shown in Fig. 3-11(b).

c. For a 90° arc in a different position, refer to the degree locations, also shown in Fig. 3-11(b). For example, the instructions to produce a semicircle in the lower portion would become:
- 180 (starting point in degrees)
- End or Return
- 360 (ending point in degrees)
- End or Return

A circle will be developed in the position shown in Fig. 3-11(c).

5. The angle of tilt can be changed. For a horizontal arc or ellipse, key in 0. For an inclined arc or ellipse, key in that number of degrees (e.g., 45). This difference is shown in Fig. 3-11(d) and (e).

6. The length of the straight line segments that form the circle can be controlled by the STEP operation. The larger the step, the less circular the object will appear. For example, a 45° instruction will yield a choppy appearing circle such as illustrated in Fig. 3-11(f). A more likely step increment for a fairly smooth-looking object would be 10 or 15° and would yield an object as seen in Fig. 3-11(g). Remember, the smaller the step, the more units of memory consumed. This limits the capability of a small micro or mini system.

7. Keying in the major and minor axes separately allows for the generation of either a circle or an ellipse. For a circle, the size instruction for the major axis is the same as for the minor axis. For an ellipse, the size instructions must be different. The size units may be inches, millimeters, or numbers that correspond to that CAD system.

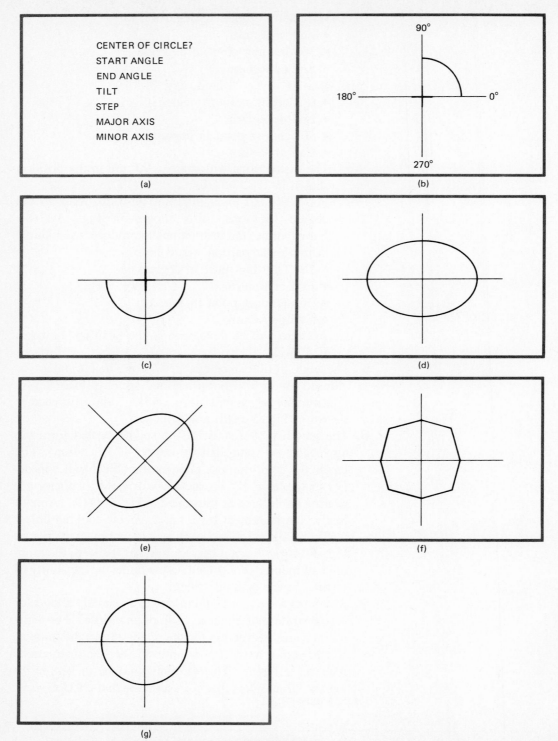

Fig. 3-11 Arc or ellipse preparation.

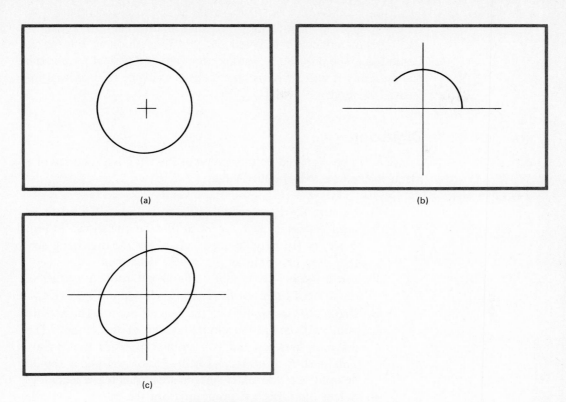

Fig. 3-12 Sample circle functions.

Examples for generating three shapes follow. The results are illustrated respectively in Fig. 3-12(a), (b), and (c).

	SHAPES		
PROMPT	**(a)**	**(b)**	**(c)**
Center or edge?	C	C	C
Starting angle (degrees)	0	0	0
Ending angle (degrees)	360	145	360
Tilt	0	0	45
Step	10	10	10
Major axis	4	4	4
Minor axis	4	4	2

A menu pad may also be used to create circles. A stylus or puck replaces the program buttons. The stylus or puck must be activated. This is accomplished by pressing it within the area CIR-

CLE. A specific manufacturer's method is illustrated in Appendix III. The manufacturer selected for this illustration is Bausch & Lomb Inc. The procedure is straightforward and typical for a menu pad system. It will serve as an excellent example of an actual industrial method.

Digitizing

A circle can be digitized on the screen of the CRT with the aid of a menu located on the graphics tablet.

1. Be sure the appropriate software is intact if a micro or mini system is used. A menu like the one shown in Fig. 3-4(a) or (b) may be used. Also, set the digitizing surface area or origin as previously described.
2. Use a stylus. Depress it on the tablet drawing surface at the desired center of the circle as shown in Fig. 3-13(a).
3. Use the stylus to digitize the second point. The second point will be on the circumference of the circle. The distance between the two points specifies the radius. This is shown in Fig. 3-13(b). Note: grid paper should be used over the tablet surface area to increase accuracy.
4. Select the CIRCLE program from the menu. Use the stylus and depress it anywhere within the area so marked. A circle will appear on the screen as shown in Fig. 3-13(c).

Hidden circles, arcs, and hidden arcs may also be generated by the above procedure. Select the HIDDEN CIRCLE, ARC, HIDDEN ARC, ARC CW (arc clockwise), or ARC CCW (arc counterclockwise) program in Step 4. A hidden circle as shown in Fig. 3-13(d) will appear on the screen after selection of the HIDDEN CIRCLE program. To produce an arc, one additional point must be digitized. Rather than digitizing the center and arc radius, digitize the center and both endpoints. Any number of solid or hidden circles or arcs may be generated on the screen. Using a puck or switching menus will vary this procedure. This is similar to that described earlier. (See also Appendix III.) Note, however, that the fundamental steps are the same and still must be executed regardless of sequence.

Certain graphics tablet menus allow a change in the step increment. Select the appropriate menu item, such as SET ROUND-

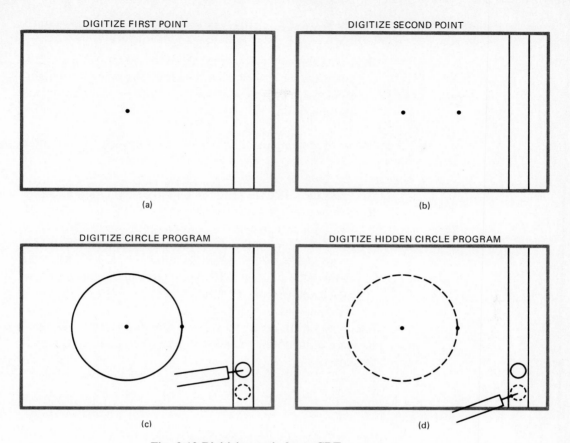

DIGITIZE FIRST POINT

(a)

DIGITIZE SECOND POINT

(b)

DIGITIZE CIRCLE PROGRAM

(c)

DIGITIZE HIDDEN CIRCLE PROGRAM

(d)

Fig. 3-13 Digitizing a circle on CRT.

NESS in Fig. 3-4(b). Next, key in the desired number of straight line steps. A 3, for example, will produce a triangle as shown in Fig. 1-3(b); a 36 will produce a circle similar to Fig. 3-11(g).

Light Pen

The light pen is used with the function board to produce a circle. It also may be used in conjunction with other devices such as the alphanumeric keyboard. One easy method that utilizes the three devices, with a known center and radius is as follows.

   1. Press the CIRCLE program button on the function board.
   2. Use the second message option SEL PT (select point) of Fig. 3-10(a). Select the desired point on the CRT using

the light pen. This point represents the center of the circle.

3. Using the keyboard, type in the desired radius (e.g., 2.0) and press the End or Return button. A circle with a diameter of 4.0 will appear on the screen, concentric to the selected point.

Another method using the light pen involves the selection of three points.

1. Press the CIRCLE program button on the function board.
2. Select each of three points on the CRT using the light pen. Each represents a location on the circumference of the circle. After you press the appropriate button, a concentric circle will appear as shown in Fig. 3-14. The radius will automatically be determined by the computer and displayed on the CRT.

A circle may be obtained by other methods, but the ones discussed here are quite common and will give you a good understanding of the basics.

3-6 Irregular Curve or Spline

An irregular curve is a nonconcentric, nonstraight line drawn smoothly through a series of points. It is commonly referred to as *spline* on CAD systems. Other nomenclature includes *smooth,*

Fig. 3-14 Three-point circle.

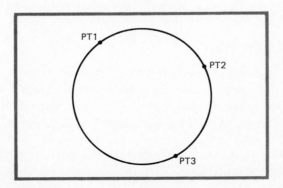

curve, and *curve fitting.* Sec. 3-5 is useful for any concentric curved geometry. Often, however, nonconcentric curves are desired. Hence, the irregular curve. The methods and procedures involve selecting several points and blending a curve through them.

Function Board and Alphanumeric Input

An alphanumeric input by itself is not used to develop the curve. It is used in conjunction with a function board, as described here.

1. Press the SPLINE (or CURVE) program button. Instructions will be displayed on the CRT. The location of a point is requested.
2. Key in X and Y coordinate values for the first point on the alphanumeric as described in Sec. 3-3, under "Alphanumeric Input." A point appears on the screen similar to Fig. 3-15(a). The instruction message changes and asks that a second point be located.
3. Repeat Step 2 for the second point. A second point appears on the screen as shown in Fig. 3-15(b). Next, the message asks for a third point location.
4. Repeat Step 2 for the third point as shown in Fig. 3-15(c). Enough information to construct a curve is now available. Additional points, however, as required may be defined as shown in Fig. 3-15(d).
5. After all the points are defined, the operation can be ended. Press the appropriate button; press the End or Return key; or type in a message. The curve tangent to each point will be displayed as shown in Fig. 3-15(e).

Keying in each point separately is an accurate but time-consuming procedure. Also, coordinate locations along a desired curve may not be known. Thus, other methods are available and may have to be used.

Digitizing

In Sec. 3-4, under "Digitizing," the graphics tablet was operating in what is known as the POINT mode. This means that as each successive point was input on the tablet, it resulted in a straight line between each. This mode must be converted to allow curved lines

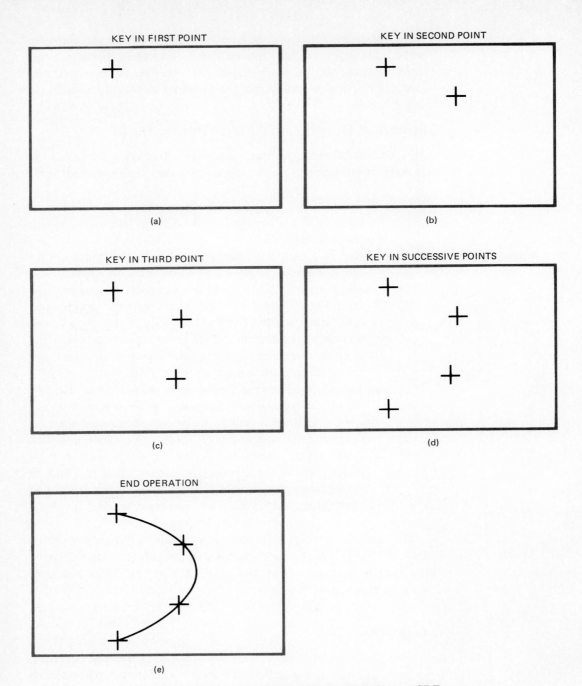

Fig. 3-15 Irregular curve (spline) generation on CRT.

to be drawn between points. This new mode is called by different names. Some manufacturers refer to it as STREAM. Changing into the mode may be as simple as pressing a button on a graphics tablet console as shown in Fig. 2-19. Another method is to select the STREAM program from a menu similar to one illustrated in Fig. 2-20. Changing to the STREAM mode means that a continuous line may be constructed rather than constructing a straight point-to-point line of a definite length.

After the mode change is complete, a curve may be developed quickly.

1. Depress the stylus, on the graphics tablet, at the location of the start of the curve. This point may be digitized from a rough sketch or perhaps from grid paper on the surface of the tablet. The network understructure senses the location.

2. Next, trace the shape of the curve with the stylus while keeping it depressed. This may be done either freehand or with the aid of a drawing instrument. The shape is duplicated and appears on the screen.

This method constructs an irregular curve as rapidly as the user can input points. Its limitation, however, is in accuracy. It is only as accurate as the user's hand and eye. This accuracy, however, is all that drawings produced by traditional drafting could ever attain.

Light Pen

A light pen may be used to construct an irregular curve directly on the CRT screen. A typical procedure follows.

1. Depress the CURVE (or SPLINE) program button on a function board. Instructions will appear for first point selection.

2. Locate the point with the light pen and press the appropriate button. The instruction message will change and ask for either a point 2 location or some other input. An example of another input would be the request that a slope be defined. Since a curve is not a straight line, the slope is equal to the tangent line of the curve at that point.

3. Locate the second point with the light pen and press the appropriate button. The instruction message will change to ask for either a point 3 location or some other input.
4. Locate the third point with the light pen and press the appropriate button. Enough information has been supplied to construct a three-point curve. Any number of additional points, however, can be added as required.
5. After all points have been defined, the procedure can be ended in a way appropriate to the particular system, for example, as described in Sec. 3-6, under "Function Board and Alphanumeric Input." The curve will appear on the screen as shown in Fig. 3-15(e).

The accuracy involved in using the light pen is similar to that of digitizing.

3-7 Dimension

Size description is the subsequent operation to shape description. This, of course, is true for any part that must be fabricated. The size of an object is described by dimensions, tolerances, symbolic representation, and notes (or text). This section deals with the foremost of these, namely dimensioning. The placement of a dimension on a drawing varies with the complexity of the available software. Some programs require you to first determine the dimensions, then use the equipment to place them on the screen. Other programs will automatically determine the dimensions with great accuracy. Next, the equipment will place the dimensions on the drawing in either fraction, decimal, or metric form or in a combination of units. This section will analyze the ways used to place dimensions on the CRT screen.

Function Board and Alphanumeric Input

A function board may be used to place a dimension on a drawing. The procedure may be simple or complex depending on the system. An extensive procedure using a smaller mini system includes the following steps.

1. Use a function board containing the following program buttons: CURSOR MOVEMENT, MOVE, LINE,

LEADER, and DIMENSION or TEXT. Use CURSOR MOVEMENT buttons to locate the cursor at the first endpoint of an extension line.

2. Press the MOVE program button.
3. Locate the cursor at the other endpoint of the extension line.
4. Press the LINE program button. An extension line will appear on the screen.
5. Repeat Steps 1 through 4 for the second extension line.
6. Repeat Steps 1 through 4 for dimension line placement. Use the LEADER (instead of the LINE) program button. The dimension line, with arrows at the extension lines, will appear on the screen.
7. Repeat Steps 1 through 4 for dimension placement. Use DIMENSION or TEXT instead of the LINE program button.
8. Type in the desired dimension (size).
9. Press End or Return. The dimension will appear on the screen.

This completes a procedure that may be used to specify the size of a part. The procedure outlined is rather extensive. It was used, however, to show you the range of variables that are considered when placing a dimension. The use of more sophisticated programs shorten the procedure considerably. You may, for example, be required to indicate each endpoint of the desired length and press one program button. The extension lines, dimension lines, and dimension will be automatically placed in the correct location.

Digitizing

Dimensions can be added to the CRT screen by digitizing. If the graphics tablet is set with the appropriate menu, a dimension may be generated. A rather extensive version of this is given here.

1. Use the stylus to digitize four points to make two lines. Follow the procedure outlined in Sec. 3-4, under "Digitizing." These lines will be located at either end of the length to be dimensioned as shown in Fig. 3-16(a). They are known as *extension lines*.

2. Next, digitize two points at the endpoints of the desired dimension line location.
3. Select the LEADER (or DIMENSION) line program from a menu similar to that shown in Fig. 3-4(a). Depending on the program arrangement, Steps 2 and 3 may have to be done twice—once at each endpoint to place an arrow at both ends. In either case, the result is shown in Fig. 3-16(b).
4. Next, digitize two points at the desired dimension location as shown in Fig. 3-16(c).
5. Select the DIMENSION (or TEXT) program from a menu using the stylus. Instructions for adding the dimension will normally appear on the screen.

Fig. 3-16 Dimensioning by digitizing.

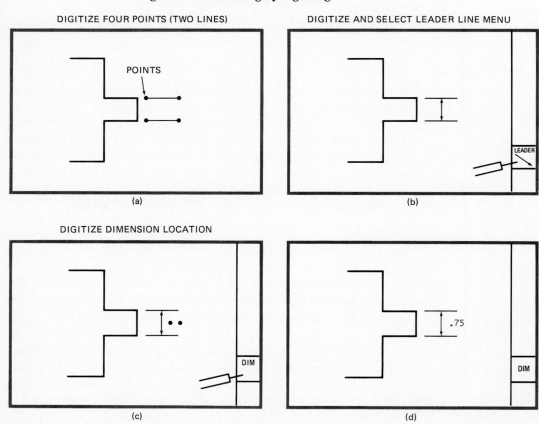

6. Using the keyboard, key in the size of the desired dimension.
7. Press End or Return. The dimension will appear on the screen similar to that shown in Fig. 3-16(d).

Additional dimensions may be added by repeating the sequence. The disadvantage of this method is that the design drafter must know the correct size. This value is manually input. Again, however, the method is no less accurate than dimensioning by the traditional means. Systems having more sophisticated software are able to sense the exact dimension and automatically display that size on the screen.

Light Pen

The light pen may be used with other pieces of equipment for different dimensioning techniques. Those analyzed in this section will be based on the use of sophisticated software. If two points on a drawing are known, the distance between them may be determined as follows.

1. Press a DIMENSION program button on a function board. Menu selection and directions will appear on the screen (or on an adjoining screen). This is similar to that shown in Fig. 3-17(a).
2. Point and activate the light pen at the desired menu choice. For example, select VT (vertical). This means that a dimension measuring a vertical distance will be displayed.
3. Select the first point with the light pen.
4. Select the second point with the light pen. These points are indicated in Fig. 3-17(b).
5. Depress the appropriate button or key to place the dimension at the location at which the light pen is pointing. Extension lines, dimension line, arrowheads, and the actual length of the dimension will be displayed. In this case, the dimension is in numeric text accurate to two decimal places. Depending on the system, accuracy may extend to six decimal places, or even beyond. Note: the dimension is automatically measured and dis-

played by the computer. The user is not required to measure, add, subtract, etc.

Another procedure, quite similar to the first, involves the selection of lines rather than points.

1. Repeat Steps 1 and 2 from the previous procedure.
2. Select the desired line using the light pen. Select one of the horizontal lines tangent to one of the points in Fig. 3-17(b).
3. Select a second horizontal line tangent to the other point in Fig. 3-17(b). Activate the light pen.
4. Depress the appropriate button or key to place the dimension at the location at which the light pen is pointing. The dimension is displayed as shown in Fig. 3-17(c) and described in Step 5 of the previous procedure.

Horizontal (HZ) or inclined (AN) dimensions may be determined by the appropriate menu selection. Either the point or the line procedure may be utilized.

Curved lines can also be automatically dimensioned. Circles, the most common curve on a typical engineering drawing, can be dimensioned in this way.

1. Repeat Step 1 of the above points procedure.
2. Select the RD (round) menu item—Fig. 3-17(a)—by pointing to and activating the light pen. The system is now in the ROUND program. Concentric curved line dimensions will be created.
3. Select the desired circle with the light pen.
4. Press the appropriate button or key to place the dimension at the location at which the light pen is pointing. The leader line, arrowhead, and the actual dimension (to two decimal places) are displayed as shown in Fig. 3-17(d).

The procedures described in this section yield extremely accurate results since the processing unit calculates the distance. Human error is eliminated. Some systems have the capability of measurement beyond six decimal places. This certainly is many times more accurate than human capability.

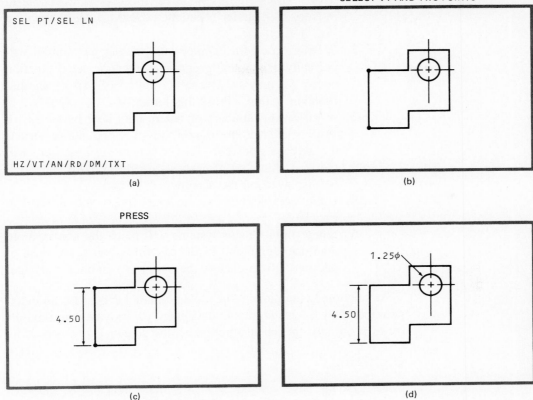

Fig. 3-17 Dimensioning with a light pen.

3-8 Text

Letters, numbers, words, notes, symbols, and messages can be inserted, as required, on an engineering drawing. These may be utilized for size description or to provide finishing touches on the drawing.

Function Board and Alphanumeric Input

The alphanumeric keyboard is used extensively for nongraphical input such as text. Messages may be composed as needed. Thus each letter or number is keyed in separately.

1. Position the cursor on the CRT screen at the desired text location. This is done by moving it about the screen with program buttons on the function board, as described in Sec. 3-4, under "Function Board," and shown in Fig. 3-7.

2. Software used for engineering drawing preparation will normally have a text program on the associated function board. It may be a separate button or part of another function button. Press this button.

3. A variety of numbers or letters may now be keyed in. With smaller programs, perhaps only one number or letter may be allowed. Larger programs, however, will allow any number of entries. Each keyboard entry will be displayed on the screen.

4. Upon completing the message, press the Return or End key.

5. Some sophisticated systems will place the text in more than one language. If this capability exists, the push of one button can change the system to another language.

As previously mentioned, the alphanumeric keyboard is an indispensable device for nongraphic data entry. It provides the flexibility to place any special instruction on the screen.

Digitizing

Many systems have a separate TEXT menu item on the graphics tablet. Others include it with DIMENSION. It depends on how the software is programmed. In either case, the general procedure includes these steps.

1. The graphics tablet must be set with the appropriate menu.

2. Digitize one or two points that correspond to the text location. This is similar to the method describing a dimension location in Sec. 3-7, under "Digitizing," and as shown in Fig. 3-16(c). (Some systems require that Step 3 below be accomplished before Step 2 is done.)

3. Select the TEXT or DIMENSION program from the menu. Use the stylus or puck and depress it anywhere within the area so represented. Instructions to add the text will appear on the screen.

4. Key in the desired text to the extent allowed by the particular system.

5. Press End or Return. The text will appear on the screen at the desired location.

All lettering will appear neatly as if produced by Leroy lettering or by a typewriter. (Leroy is a registered trademark of Kueffel & Esser Co.) You now have the ability to letter a drawing without having to develop lettering technique. Additionally, the height, font (or lettering style), and the language may be changed. Flexibility depends on the sophistication of the programming.

Light Pen

The light pen may be used, with or without an alphanumeric keyboard, to place text on the CRT. A typical procedure includes the following.

1. Select the appropriate button on the function board. It may be titled TEXT or be contained under some other label, such as MISC. A set of instructions will appear on the screen. An example is shown in Fig. 3-18(a).

2. Use the light pen to select the NOTE menu item.

3. The position of the note may be determined by the instructions across the top of the screen. For example, the alphanumeric keyboard may be used to key in this location. The light pen may also be used for selection. Normally, the accuracy of location of a note is not critical; thus, light pen selection will suffice. The instructions at

Fig. 3-18 Text menu and prompt display on CRT.

```
KEY X, Y/SEL PT/SEL NOTE




NOTE/ARW/
```
(a)

```
SEL TEXT/KEY TEXT/LARGE NOTE




```
(b)

the top of the screen will change. An example is shown in Fig. 3-18(b).

4. Once again, we see that either the light pen or keyboard may be used to produce the note. By using the SEL TXT (select text) message instruction, the note may be selected. If no text is available from the menu, text may be keyed in by means of the keyboard.

5. Depress the End or Return button. The text appears at the desired location.

3-9 Geometry Modifiers

A variety of geometry modification commands are available. Depending on the system, they may be referred to quite differently. Large systems generally have a selection of commands, and the commands are complex. No matter how many there are or how complex they are, all geometry modifiers are used to complete an engineering drawing. One geometry modification command will be covered in this section. Other specialized functions will be further elaborated on in Chap. 5.

Perhaps you may desire to alter the length of an element that appears on the screen. The element may be a line, a circle, an arc, an ellipse, a spline, or text. A command to do this might be known as CHANGE, ALTER, or RELIMIT, among other terms. The procedure involves the following.

1. Select the appropriate program button on the function board. Instructions will appear on the screen. They may be used to make an element either longer or shorter or to break an element into more than one segment.

2. Select the menu item for changing the length of an element. This may be done with the light pen. One manufacturer refers to this item as ENDS.

3. Next, identify the end of the element to be modified. If it is a line, select, using the light pen, anywhere between the center and the end of the line to modify it. This is shown in Fig. 3-19.

4. Use the light pen to indicate the position that the element is to be modified to. Indicating beyond the existing line will lengthen the line. Modifying may include lengthening as well as shortening the line end.

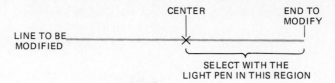

Fig. 3-19 Modify the length of a line.

Summary

There are basic functions common to all engineering drawings. These include shape and size description. In the preparation of an engineering drawing on the screen of a CRT, basic functions must be executed. The basic functions (e.g., to draw a line) are objects of commands. Drafting terminology often refer to these functions as *commands*. They may be recalled by the touch of a button on a device known as a *function board*. A function board may be referred to by other names. Some of these include *program function keyboard, function keyboard, command board,* and *menu tablet or pad*. A function board may be used with one or more other pieces of CAD equipment. The common pieces of peripheral equipment are:

- Alphanumeric keyboard.
- Joystick or thumbwheels.
- Graphics tablet.
- Light pen.

This chapter covered a broad sampling of several common methods used to create an image on the CRT screen, including graphic and nongraphic data entry. The procedures vary somewhat from manufacturer to manufacturer. You may be required, for example, to press an extra button or add a step in the procedure. However, the principles required to create a basic engineering drawing remain the same regardless of the specific type of equipment used.

Terms to Know

A	Ampere. Unit of electrical current. One ampere will flow through one ohm resistance at one volt potential difference.
AWG	American wire gage. A standardized series of wire conductor diameters. A no. 14 gage is the commercial minimum size allowed.
Axis	Distance from one side of an ellipse or arc to the opposite side 180° apart. There is a *major axis* and a *minor axis*.

Command	A series of directions used to execute a function on a CAD system.
Concentric	Having a common center such as a circle or ellipse.
Current	The rate or amount of electricity flowing. It is measured in units of amperes.
Font	A certain style and size of type.
Function	Produce a change in the display on a CRT screen. For example, adding a line or text.
Geometry modifier or manipulator	A function used to alter a drawing on the CRT screen. For example, shortening the length of a line is considered a geometry modifier or manipulator.
Grid	Bright dots on the CRT screen spaced to form a square pattern.
Increment	See *step*.
Mode	A part of a computer that allows the user to perform a certain type of function as *point mode*.
Power	The rate of expending energy. The unit watt (W) is used to describe electrical energy.
Program button	Located on a function board. Pressing a button (e.g., LINE) connects the software program enabling that function (e.g., draw a line) to be performed.
Spline	A common term used to describe the irregular curve concept in conventional drafting.
Step	A discrete function. A definite length or distance.
Tilt	The angle at which an object is turned. It is normally measured in degrees.
V	Volt. The unit of electrical energy or potential.
W	Watt. A unit of electrical power.

Questions

1. What is the difference between a command and a function?
2. Where do written instructions or prompts appear?
3. What is the primary purpose of a prompt?
4. Where is the POINT button located?
5. What is the effect of pressing the alphanumeric Return key?
6. What is the purpose of the function board buttons?
7. How can absolute, or exact, coordinates be placed on the screen?
8. What does the cursor do?
9. What are the coordinate values of an origin?

10. Must the cursor be repositioned when you are drawing additional circles around a common center? Explain.

11. What values are entered to draw an absolute half circle? Begin the arc at three o'clock (right).

12. Explain why a circle is not drawn by a continuous curved line. Refer to the procedure outlined in Sec. 3-5, under "Function Board and Alphanumeric Input."

13. How does data entry differ for circle and ellipse creation?

14. How is a spline developed by a graphics tablet?

15. Why does spline not fall within the circle category as do arc and ellipse?

16. Why is the user not required to measure or calculate a dimension with many CAD systems?

17. What piece of equipment is most important for text entry?

Problems

The following problems may be solved either with or without the use of CAD equipment. Simulations of an alphanumeric keyboard and a function board can be used. The answers will be expressed in chart form rather than on a CRT screen. Each grid square in the figures is 0.12 long. The X-Y zero axis is located at the lower left of each figure.

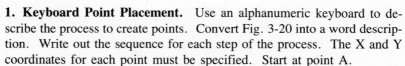

Fig. 3-20

1. Keyboard Point Placement. Use an alphanumeric keyboard to describe the process to create points. Convert Fig. 3-20 into a word description. Write out the sequence for each step of the process. The X and Y coordinates for each point must be specified. Start at point A.

Prepare a chart for each point location using the following format.

POINT	X COORDINATE	Y COORDINATE
Identify each point: e.g., A.	Location	Location

2. Function Board Point Placement. Use a function board to describe the process to create points. Use a board with a POINT program button. Convert Fig. 3-20 into a word description. Write out the sequence for each step of the process. The X and Y coordinates for each point must be located. Start at point A. Each press of the cursor movement buttons will move it 0.12 (the distance between one square grid).

Prepare a chart to locate each point using the following format.

POINT	PARTIAL PROCESS
Identify each point: e.g., A.	Initial cursor position. Press MOVE program button. Press cursor movement button(s) ? times. Press POINT program button.

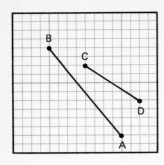

Fig. 3-21

3. Keyboard Line Placement. Use an alphanumeric keyboard to describe the process to create lines. Convert Fig. 3-21 into a word description. Write out the sequence for each step of the process. The X and Y coordinates for each line must be specified. You should start at point A.

Prepare a chart for each line endpoint location using the following format.

LINE	X COORDINATE	Y COORDINATE
Identify each line endpoint: e.g., A.	Location	Location

4. Function Board Line Placement. Use a function board to describe the process to create lines. Use a board with a LINE button. Convert drawing Fig. 3-21 into a word description. Write out the sequence for each step of the process. The X and Y coordinates for each line must be located. Start at point A. Each press of the cursor movement buttons will move it 0.12 (the distance between one square grid).

Prepare a chart to locate each line using the following format.

LINE	PARTIAL PROCESS
Identify each line: e.g., AB.	Initial cursor position. Press MOVE program button. Press cursor movement button(s) ? times. Press POINT program button.

5. Function Board and Keyboard Circle Generation. Use a function board and an alphanumeric keyboard to describe the process to create a circle. Convert Fig. 3-22 into a word description. Write out the sequence for the process. The center, radius, and angle of arc must be indicated. Start at the center.

Prepare a chart for the circle using the following format.

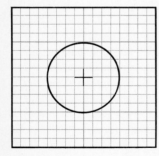

Fig. 3-22

CIRCLE	PROCESS
Identify the object.	Position the cursor. Press CIRCLE program button. Key in desired radius. Key in start angle. Key in end angle. Press End or Return key.

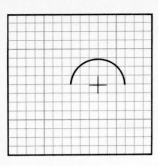

Fig. 3-23

6. Function Board and Keyboard Arc Generation. Repeat the process that was outlined in Problem 5 on page 98, except create the arc shown in Fig. 3-23.

7. Function Board and Keyboard Spline Generation. Use a function board and an alphanumeric keyboard to describe the process to create a spline. Convert Fig. 3-24 into a word description. Write out the sequence for the process. At least five points on the curve must be indicated.

Prepare a chart for the process using the following format.

POINT	PARTIAL PROCESS
Identify each point on the curve.	Press SPLINE program button. Key in X and Y coordinates.

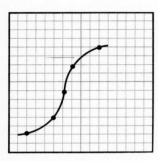

Fig. 3-24

8. Function Board and Keyboard Text Placement. Use a function board and alphanumeric keyboard to describe the process to place text. Convert Fig. 3-25 into a word description. Write out the sequence for the process.

Prepare a chart for the process using the following format:

TEXT	PARTIAL PROCESS
Identify each label.	Position the cursor. Press TEXT program button. Key in label. Press End or Return.

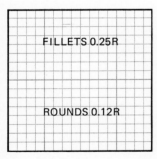

FILLETS 0.25R

ROUNDS 0.12R

Fig. 3-25

9. Shape and Size Generation Using a Function Board and Keyboard. Repeat Problems 1 through 8 as assigned by your instructor. Use additional figures from a traditional drafting text for each assignment.

10. Basic Functions Using a Graphics Tablet Menu. Repeat Problems 2, 4, 5, 6, 7, and 8 with Figs. 3-20 through 3-25. Replace the method of using a function board with a menu. Use the menu shown in Fig. 3-4.

11. Shape and Size Generation Using a Graphics Tablet Menu. Repeat problems described in Problem 10 above as assigned by your instructor. Use additional figures from a traditional drafting text for each assignment.

12. Basic Functions Using a Light Pen. Repeat Problems 2, 4, 5, 7, and 8 with Figs. 3-20, 3-21, 3-22, 3-24, and 3-25. Replace the use of a function board with a light pen method. Follow the procedure for each method described in this chapter.

13. Shape and Size Generation Using a Light Pen. Repeat problems described in Problem 12 above as assigned by your instructor. Use additional figures from a traditional drafting text for each assignment.

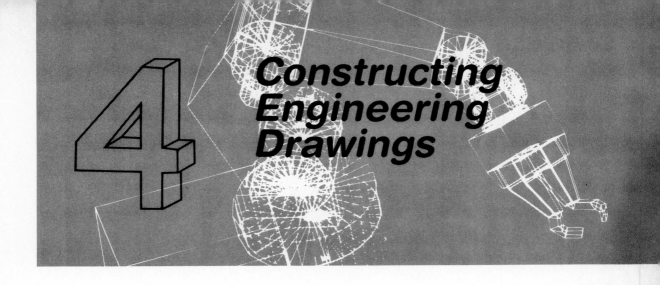

Constructing Engineering Drawings

4-1 Introduction

This chapter will show applications for the creation of engineering drawings. Before proceeding, you will need a basic knowledge of drafting. The principles of engineering drawing and drafting must be understood. These include multiview projection, sectioning, auxiliary views, pictorials, dimensioning, tolerancing, symbolic representation, and the reading and understanding of schematic diagrams.

Chapter 2 introduced the common types of CAD equipment. It covered the functions of each major piece. Next, the basic graphics and nongraphics essential to engineering drawing preparation were developed. Each Chap. 3 data-entry procedure comprised one entry on a drawing. Now that you understand how to execute each, several will be combined. They will be used in conjunction with different pieces of equipment to produce drawings.

The combination of the procedures and equipment enable you to produce an unlimited variety of drawings. The following common ways to accomplish this will be dealt with in this chapter.

- Mechanical drawing using a function board.
- Schematic diagram using a function board.
- Mechanical drawing using a graphics tablet.
- Piping diagram using a graphics tablet.
- Mechanical drawing using a light pen.
- Symbol development using a joystick.

A CAD system with at least 32K bytes of memory (preferably more) should be used. Each of the drawings, while not extensive, will require a memory of this magnitude. If a small system is used, it will only be "good until the last byte."

**4-2
Mechanical
Drawing
Using a
Function
Board**

A mechanical drawing such as the one shown in Fig. 4-1(k) can be generated on the CRT screen with a function board. The board must contain the program buttons used to execute each basic procedure described in Chap. 3. A sample board is shown in Fig. 4-1(a). Each button will be connected to a program and used to accomplish a particular command. By combining various mechanical drawing commands, you can create an engineering drawing. A procedure to prepare the shape of an object on the screen is given here.

1. First, make sure the system is activated. Program buttons 2, 5, 7, and 10 shown in Fig. 4-1(a) are used to position the cursor.
2. After the initial endpoint has been positioned, press the MOVE button, 11. The cursor will be positioned as shown in Fig. 4-1(b).
3. Next, press 7 enough times to move the cursor to the other endpoint.
4. Press the LINE program button, 3. The first line appears on the screen as shown in Fig. 4-1(c).
5. Continue repositioning the cursor with horizontal or vertical buttons 2, 5, 7, and 10. Press the LINE button each time the cursor is positioned at the desired endpoint of a line. A series of horizontal and vertical lines, such as shown in Fig. 4-1(d), are constructed.
6. To draw a diagonal line, combine horizontal and vertical movements. Press 2 or 10 and a vertical move is made. Press 5 or 7 and a horizontal move is made. (Refer to Sec. 3-4 for further explanation.) Remember, after positioning the cursor in the initial position, press the MOVE button. This signals the processor that you do not intend a continuation of a previous line.
7. After the cursor is positioned at the second endpoint,

press the LINE button. An inclined line, as shown in Fig. 4-1(e), will appear on the screen.

8. Repeat Steps 6 and 7 for the other inclined line. The result is shown in Fig. 4-1(f).

9. An arc may be constructed. First, position the cursor to the center of the arc.

10. Press the CIRCLE program button, 9.

11. Follow the instructions on the screen. Respond to each prompt by providing input data using the keyboard.

Fig. 4-1 Mechanical drawing using a function board.

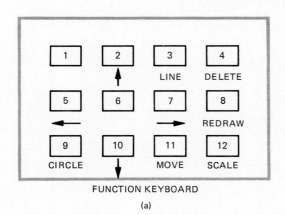

FUNCTION KEYBOARD

(a)

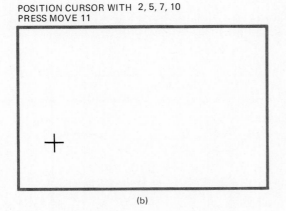

POSITION CURSOR WITH 2, 5, 7, 10
PRESS MOVE 11

(b)

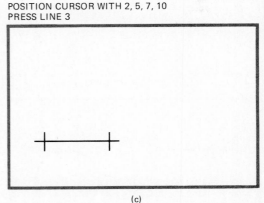

POSITION CURSOR WITH 2, 5, 7, 10
PRESS LINE 3

(c)

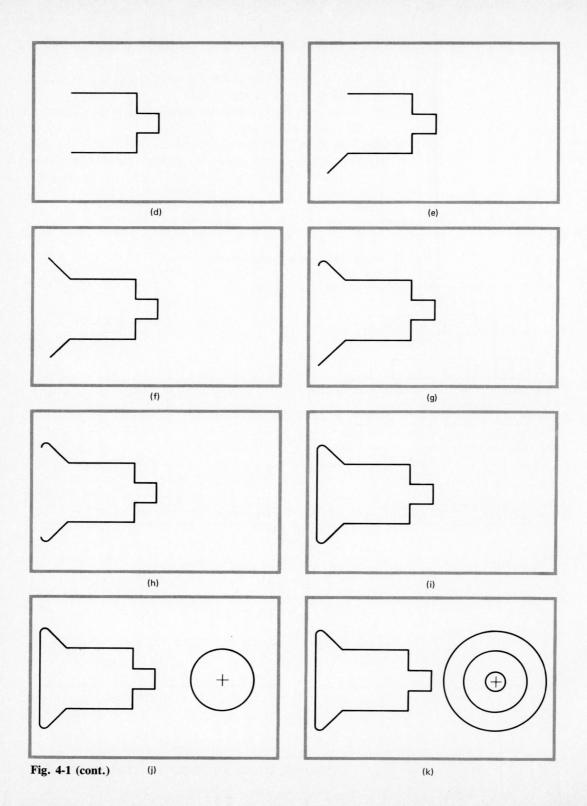

Fig. 4-1 (cont.)
(d) (e) (f) (g) (h) (i) (j) (k)

PROMPT	RESPONSE	MEANING
Center or edge?	C	Yes, cursor is at the center of the desired arc. (E would indicate the edge.)
Starting angle (degrees)	90	Arc will begin at north position.
Ending angle (degrees)	180	Curve is to extend counterclockwise from 90 to 180°. Remember, 0° is at the horizontal right and increases counterclockwise.
Tilt (degrees)	0	No angle from the horizontal
Step (degrees)	10	Circumference of arc is drawn with straight line increments every 10°.
Major axis	0.75	
Minor axis	0.75	Arc will be concentric with a 0.75 radius.

Note: an extensive series of prompts have been used for this example in order to include the full range of parameters that are considered. The use of more sophisticated programs, however, will simplify curved line generation. For example, some systems require only that the center and radius be defined.

12. After data entry, press the appropriate button. An arc as shown in Fig. 4-1(g) will appear on the screen.

13. Repeat Steps 10, 11, and 12 for a second arc. Change the position of the cursor to the center of the new arc and extend the curve from 180 to 270°. The arc, as shown in Fig. 4-1(h), will appear on the screen.

14. The front view of the object is completed by one additional vertical line. Repeat Steps 2, 3, and 4 except use the vertical direction buttons 2 and 10 to position the second endpoint. The front view of the object is shown in Fig. 4-1(i).

15. Next, the right side view may be constructed. Reposition the cursor to the center of desired location of the view. Use program buttons 2, 5, 7, and 10.

16. Press the CIRCLE program button, 9. Note: some systems may additionally require pressing MOVE. This allows cursor movement to a new view without the drawing of a line.

17. Follow the instructions on the screen. Provide input data concerning the circle such as:
   a. Cursor is at the center (key Yes).
   b. Circle is to extend from 0 to 360°.
   c. Step (e.g., 10° straight line increments) and tilt (0°) data.
   d. Size of the major and minor axes (e.g., 1.50).
18. After data input, press the appropriate button. A circle, as shown in Fig. 4-1(j), will appear on the screen.
19. Repeat Steps 16, 17, and 18 for the second and third circles. Change the major and minor axes to correspond to the front view (e.g., 0.75 and 2.25). The right side view will appear as shown in Fig. 4-1(k).

This completes the procedure for developing the shape description of an object using a function board. It will vary somewhat with different manufacturer equipment. Note the difference, for example, between procedures in Appendix I and Appendix III. After completing the drawing on the screen, you can either make a copy or store the drawing on a file for future use. If a copy is desired, enter one more instruction using the function board or keyboard to signal to the output equipment and a finished drawing will be produced.

4-3 Schematic Diagram Using a Function Board

Various schematic diagrams [Fig. 4-2(j)] may be constructed on the screen using a function board. Common ones include electrical, electronic, and piping diagrams. A diagram may consist of a small number of symbols. Each may have to be displayed several times. Consequently, programs have been developed to draw each of the standard symbols. A press of the correct button or key will call up the graphic representation of a component. The button or key may be either on a function board or on the alphanumeric. Having a developed program for each standard symbol eliminates the time-consuming repetitive preparation of individual symbols. It becomes possible to instantly create any number of standard symbols on the screen. This process, known as *step and repeat,* is yet another significant time-saving benefit of CAD.

An electronic diagram will be prepared as an illustration of schematic procedure. A basic knowledge of electronic schematic diagrams should first be acquired by the user. For this illustration, each of the symbols will be called upon on the screen by a function board program button. A corresponding alphanumeric key procedure, where different, will be indicated in parentheses. A sample board is shown in Fig. 4-2(a). Only a few of the standard electronic symbols needed to prepare this diagram have been included. Others, such as NPN transistors, inductors, and so on, may also be used. Program buttons corresponding to these would be included on the board.

The procedure is as follows.

1. First, make sure the system is activated.
2. Program buttons 2, 6, 8, and 12 from Fig. 4-2(a) are used to position the cursor. After the starting point has been positioned, press the START POINT button, 1.
3. Next press buttons 2, 6, 8, or 12 enough times to move the cursor to the next position.
4. To fix the starting point and endpoint for a symbol or line, press the ENDPOINT program button, 11.
5. If you wish to first draw a line, press the LINE program button, 3. A line will appear on the screen, as shown in Fig. 4-2(b). (If the alphanumeric is used rather than a function board, this step of the procedure changes. You key in the space bar and press End or Return.)
6. For a second line, repeat Steps 2, 3, 4, and 5. A second line appears on the screen, as shown in Fig. 4-2(c).
7. If you wish to place a resistor symbol at the top end of the second line, first repeat Steps 2, 3, and 4.
8. To place the symbol within this location, press the RES (resistor) program button, 14. (On the alphanumeric, key in R and press End or Return.) The symbol will be displayed as shown in Fig. 4-2(d).
9. If you wish to place a PNP transistor symbol at the bottom end of the second line, first repeat Steps 2, 3, and 4.
10. To place the symbol within this location, press the PNP TRANS program button, 10. (On the alphanumeric, key in P and press End or Return.) The symbol will be displayed as shown in Fig. 4-2(e).

11. Continue this procedure. Another line can be generated by the repetition of Steps 2, 3, 4, and 5.
12. To place a capacitor symbol at the right end of the new line, repeat Steps 2, 3, and 4.
13. To place the symbol within this location, press the CAP (capacitor) program button, 5. (On the alphanumeric, key in C and press End or Return.) The previous line and the capacitor symbol will be displayed as shown in Fig. 4-2(f).
14. You may continue to add lines and symbols in any desired location by repeating Steps 2 through 13. A variation in the sequence of the steps may be used, depending on the order of symbols and how they are to be connected. For example, it may be necessary to place a resistor, a line, a PNP transistor, a line, and a resistor, in that order. The sequence of procedure steps would be as follows: 2, 3, 4, and 8 (resistor); 2, 3, 4, and 5 (line); 2, 3, 4, and 10 (PNP transistor); 2, 3, 4, and 5 (line); 2, 3, 4, and 8 (resistor).
15. After all necessary lines, resistors, PNP transistors, and capacitors have been drawn, the screen display will appear as shown in Fig. 4-2(g).
16. The layout of this electronic diagram, known as a flip-flop circuit, may be completed by the addition of a ground symbol. First repeat Steps 2, 3, and 4 at the desired location.
17. To place the symbol, press the GROUND program button, 15. (On the alphanumeric, key in E and press End or Return.) The completed flip-flop connected circuit will appear as shown in Fig. 4-2(h).
18. Next, text may be added to the diagram. The text on an electronic diagram is used to:
    a. Uniquely identify each component.
    b. Specify the size or capacity of each component.
    c. Specify the input and output.
    First determine the text location. Next, repeat Steps 2, 3, and 4 at the specified location.
19. Press the LABEL program button, 13.
20. To label the size of a capacitor, key in the desired text (e.g., 220 pF). Press the End or Return key. The text will appear on the screen as shown in Fig. 4-2(i).

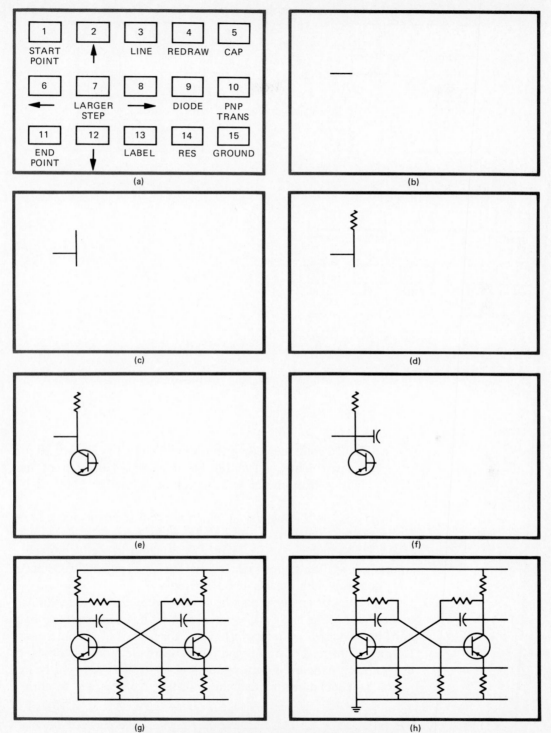

Fig. 4-2 Schematic diagram using a function board.

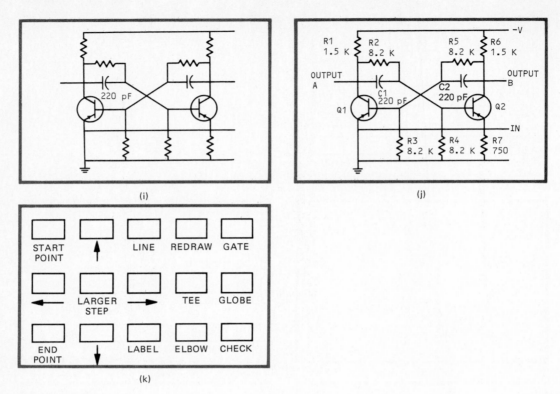

Fig. 4-2 (cont.)

21. To continue adding text, repeat Steps 18, 19, and 20 for each entry. The finished schematic diagram of the flip-flop circuit will appear as shown in Fig. 4-2(j).

Depending on the manner in which the line segments have been drawn on this schematic, a system with more than a 32K memory is required. Remember, keep each line segment as long as possible. Create a long line rather than several shorter segments since each new step uses additional bytes of memory.

Schematics of any type may be developed by a procedure similar to the above. The appropriate software must be used, and the menu must be switched. A piping schematic diagram, for example, may be drawn. Instead of a program for standard electronic symbols, a program for standard piping symbols is used. The function board button nomenclature (or alphanumeric keys) is changed to correspond. Some CAD systems use a removable mask over the function board. The menu may be switched with each software change, and the buttons then correspond to the new program. A typical mask is shown in Fig. 4-2(k). Note: complete schematics may be drawn without the lettering or line technique skill required by conventional drafting.

4-4 Mechanical Drawing Using a Graphics Tablet

A drawing [Fig. 4-3(p)] can be generated on the CRT screen by digitizing. If a menu similar to that shown in Fig. 3-4(a) is available, each item may be quickly selected. The complete procedure includes the following steps.

1. First, make sure the system is activated and the software is set for digitizing.
2. Next, set the digitizing area. This is normally accomplished by following instructions on the screen. Generally, it involves depressing a stylus to indicate the corners of the surface. This is shown by the four dots in Fig. 4-3(a).
3. Digitize two points on the surface and select the LINE menu. Do this by depressing the stylus at the three positions. A line will appear on the screen as shown in Fig. 4-3(b).
4. Repeat Step 3 for each object line in the top view. The result is shown in Fig. 4-3(c).
5. Digitize two points on the surface and select the HIDDEN LINE menu. A dotted line will appear on the screen as shown in Fig. 4-3(d).
6. Repeat Step 5 for each hidden line in the top view. This is shown in Fig. 4-3(e).
7. Digitize two points on the surface and select the CIRCLE menu. The two points will correspond to the center of the circle and its radius. A circle as shown in Fig. 4-3(f) will appear on the screen.
8. Repeat Step 7 for each circle in the top view. This is shown in Fig. 4-3(g).
9. Digitize two points on the surface and select the CENTER LINE menu. A center line will appear on the screen as shown in Fig. 4-3(h).

10. Repeat Step 9 for each center line in the top view. The shape description of the top view is now complete and is shown in Fig. 4-3(i).

11. Next, move to the front view located directly below the top. Digitize three points and select the ARC menu. The points will correspond to the beginning of the arc, center of the arc, and end of the arc. An arc as shown in Fig. 4-3(j) will be displayed on the screen.

12. Repeat Steps 3, 4, 5, 6, 9, and 10 as required for the front view. These will draw the object lines, hidden lines, and center lines. The complete front view is shown in Fig. 4-3(k).

13. Next, move to the right side view. It is located to the right of, and at the same elevation as, the front view. Repeat Steps 3, 4, 5, 6, 9, and 10 as required for this view. The object, hidden, and center lines will be drawn. This completes the shape description of the object. The object, known as a shaft support, is shown in Fig. 4-3(1).

14. Next, the shaft support can be dimensioned. This portion of the procedure is lengthy, and the results are accurate only to the extent of the design drafter's ability. The complete procedure will be used in this section. This way you will see every parameter involved in dimensioning. Remember, the more sophisticated the program used, the less complicated the input procedure.

    To place a dimension on the screen requires completing the seven-step procedure explained in Sec. 3-7, under "Digitizing." This must be done for each dimension. As the procedure explains, operations must be performed to:

    a. Digitize two lines (four points) for the extension lines.

    b. Digitize a leader line (or two, depending on the program) for the dimension.

    c. Digitize two points to locate the dimension.

    d. Digitize and key in the dimension.

    Refer to Sec. 3-7, under "Digitizing," for an amplified version of these operations. After you complete this procedure within a procedure, the dimension will appear as shown in Fig. 4-3(m).

15. Repeat Step 14 for each remaining two-point dimension. The result is shown in Fig. 4-3(n).

16. Arcs and diameters can next be dimensioned as follows.

    a. Digitize two points and the leader menu. The leader extends from the edge of the circle to outside the object.

    b. Digitize two points and the line menu. The line extends from the end of the leader and the start of the size.

    c. Digitize two points and the dimension menu. The two points locate dimension placement.

    d. Key in the desired dimension size using the alphanumeric. Press End or Return.

    e. Repeat Steps 16c and 16d above if two lines of size information are necessary.

    After you complete these steps, a diameter or arc will be dimensioned as shown in Fig. 4-3(o).

17. Complete diameter and arc dimensioning by repeating Step 16 for each. The complete size and shape description for the shaft support is shown in Fig. 4-3(p).

18. Any additional notes or text may be added to the drawing. If necessary, refer to the procedure outlined in Sec. 3-8, under ''Digitizing.''

Fig. 4-3 Mechanical drawing using a graphics tablet.

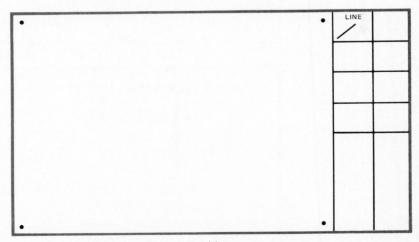

(a)

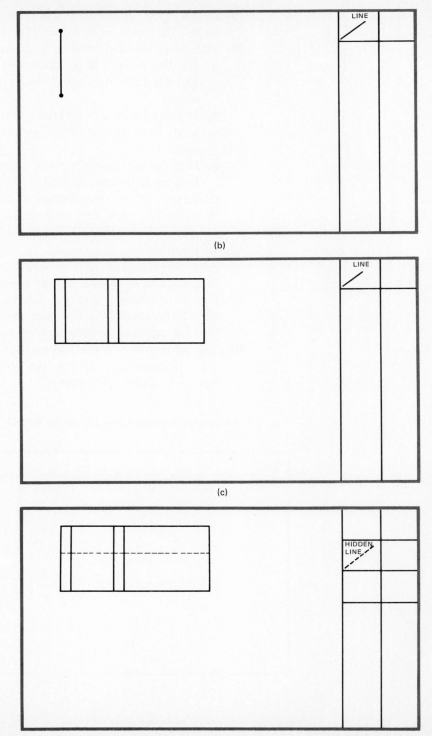

(b)

(c)

Fig. 4-3 (cont.)

(d)

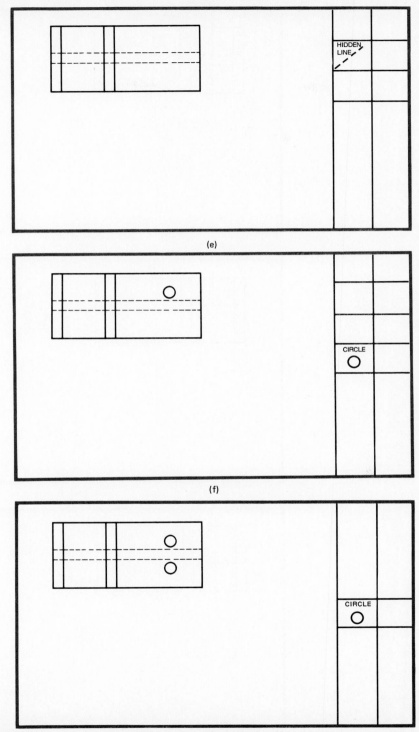

(e)

(f)

(g)

Fig. 4-3 (cont.)

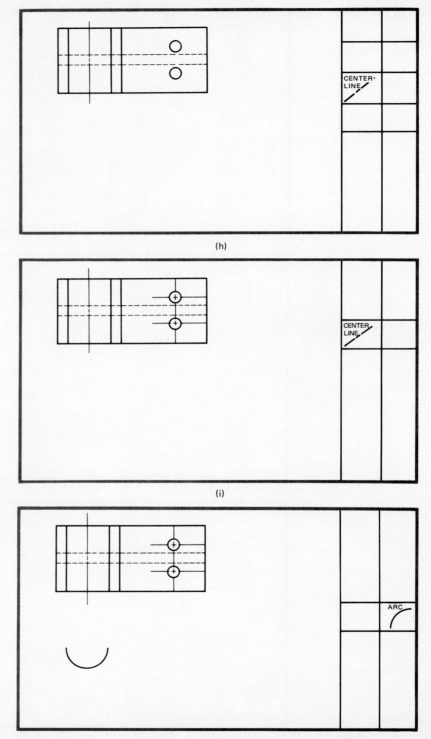

Fig. 4-3 (cont.)

(h)

(i)

(j)

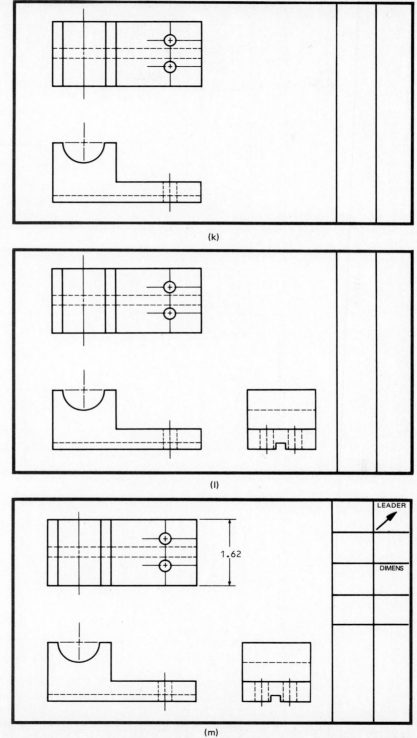

(k)

(l)

1.62

LEADER

DIMENS

(m)

Fig. 4-3 (cont.)

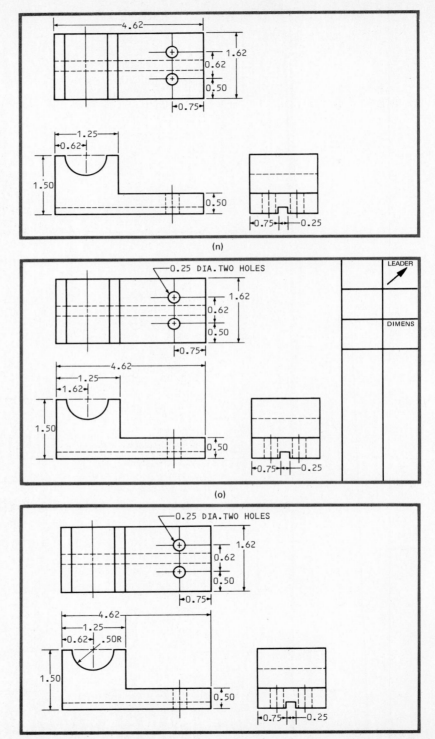

(n)

0.25 DIA.TWO HOLES

LEADER

DIMENS

(o)

0.25 DIA.TWO HOLES

Fig. 4-3 (cont.)

(p)

This completes the procedure used to prepare an engineering or a detail drawing by digitizing. It may be used for virtually any drawing made up of lines, arcs, dimensions, and text. The shape description is completed rapidly. The size description requires considerably more time using a small system. Once the drawing is complete, a copy can be made or the drawing can be filed for future recall.

4-5 Piping Diagram Using a Graphics Tablet

A schematic diagram [Fig. 4-4(d)] can be prepared by digitizing. The manner is similar to that presented in Sec. 4-3. The difference lies with the use of a menu. For a piping schematic, all standard piping symbols must be included. A typical partial menu of several valves may appear similar to that shown in Fig. 4-4(a). Instead of its being on a function board or menu pad, the menu accompanies the graphics tablet. Also, it can be changed to accommodate other symbols by a process referred to as *menu switching*. An example of menu switching is illustrated by the menu pad shown in Appendix III. The two columns at the left of the menu are standard items. These have been explained and utilized in previous sections. The remaining three columns contain piping symbols. While these are the standard flanged symbols, others, such as threaded or welded ones, may readily be used. The menu can be switched and coordinated with the software. The top row of the menu shown includes three different gate valves; the second row, three types of globe valves; the third row, three types of check valves. Other various symbols are included on the final row.

The following procedure is used to prepare the drawing.

1. First, make sure the system is activated and set for digitizing.
2. Next, set the digitizing area as previously described.
3. To place a line on the screen, digitize two points with a stylus on the graphics tablet surface. The points correspond to the desired location.
4. Next, select the LINE menu by using the stylus. A line will be placed on the screen.
5. A symbol may be placed on the screen. First, repeat Step 3. Any symbol may be drawn either left to right, or right

to left, depending on the order in which the two points are digitized. Next, select the desired symbol item. For example, if a gate valve is desired, use the stylus to select the right-most box on the top row. The result is shown in Fig. 4-4(b).

6. Any number of lines, symbols, circles, or arcs may be placed on the screen. Repeat Step 3 and select the appropriate menu items. A process and instrumentation diagram (P & ID) may appear similar to that shown in Fig. 4-4(c).

7. The diagram may be finished by adding internal parts and text. You can add internal parts (e.g., trays) by repeating Step 3 and selecting the HIDDEN LINE menu. Add words by repeating Step 3 and selecting the TEXT menu. The complete P & ID is shown in Fig. 4-4(d).

This procedure, used to prepare a piping diagram, was presented in an abbreviated manner. Each minute instruction was not given because of the detailed coverage in previous sections. An illustrative example is presented in Appendix IV. Instead of using a valve symbol menu, however, the user generated each line separately. The rough sketch of a piping isometric was placed on the tablet surface. The procedure actually became a continuation of Appendix I.

Other types of schematics may be prepared by digitizing and by using the menu switching concept previously mentioned. The software must be changed to correspond to the new menu card. To develop, for example, industrial electrical control diagrams, you would use a menu similar to that shown in Fig. 4-4(e). Pressing the appropriate button would switch the software.

Fig. 4-4 Piping diagram using a graphics tablet.

PARTIAL MENU FOR PIPING DIAGRAM
(a)

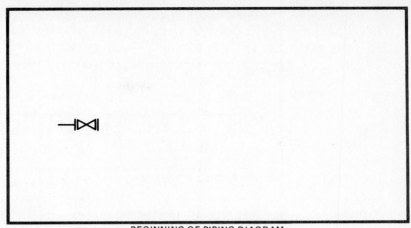

BEGINNING OF PIPING DIAGRAM
(b)

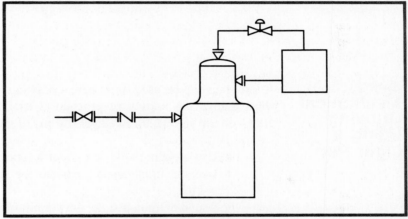

PIPING DIAGRAM OBJECT LINES
(c)

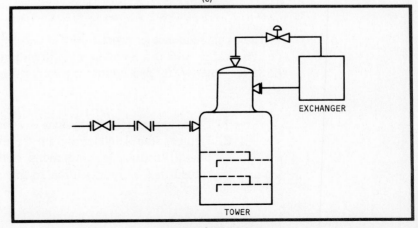

COMPLETED P & ID
(d)

Fig. 4-4 (cont.)

LINE	DIMEN			
HIDDEN LINE	TEXT			
CIRCLE	ARC			
HIDDEN CIRCLE	HIDDEN ARC			

PARTIAL MENU FOR ELECTRICAL CONTROL SCHEMATIC

Fig. 4-4 (cont.)

(e)

4-6 Mechanical Drawing Using a Light Pen

A light pen can be used to prepare a drawing [Fig. 4-5(e)] in many ways due to the variety of procedures available. A line may be drawn on the screen, for example, by any of the following methods.

- Use alphanumeric key input to specify the length.
- Use the light pen to indicate the first and second endpoints.
- Use the light pen to draw unlimited length lines, then shorten each line.

The exact sequence or procedure will depend upon the individual design drafter and the amount of information available. Briefly, however, one typical procedure may be performed in the following sequence.

1. First, make sure the system is activated.
2. Depress the LINE program button on the function board. Instructions and menu options appear on the screen in a fashion similar to that shown in Fig. 3-9.

3. Use the light pen to select HORIZ (horizontal lines) from the menu across the bottom of the screen.

4. Follow the procedure outlined in Sec. 3-4, under "Light Pen," for the desired horizontal lines having an unlimited length.

5. Next, use the light pen to select VERT (vertical lines) from the menu across the bottom of the screen.

6. Repeat Step 4 for the desired vertical lines having an unlimited length. The screen will appear as shown in Fig. 4-5(a). For clarity, the outline of the object is shown darker.

7. Change the length of each line as outlined by the procedure in Sec. 3-9. The picture on the screen is altered to that shown in Fig. 4-5(b). It represents the lines of a three-view engineering drawing.

8. Solid lines may be changed to hidden or dashed lines. Press the appropriate program button (i.e., TYPE or DASH). Use the light pen to select the hidden line menu item; then select the appropriate line. The screen is altered to that shown in Fig. 4-5(c).

9. Circles may be added to the drawing by following the procedure outlined in Sec. 3-5, under "Light Pen."

10. Center lines are drawn by a procedure similar to that used to draw horizontal and vertical object lines. Select CTR (center line) from the menu across the bottom of the screen. The drawing (with the addition of circles and center lines) appears as shown in Fig. 4-5(d). This completes the shape description.

11. Each dimension may be added by following one of the light pen procedures outlined in Sec. 3-7. The complete size and shape description of the object is shown in Fig. 4-5(e).

This completes one procedure that may be used to describe the shape and size of an object. Many variations of the procedure may be used to produce the same result. The method used will depend largely upon the user's experience. At any rate, an engineering drawing has been prepared. Once again, line technique and lettering skills are not required. An added feature of the light pen

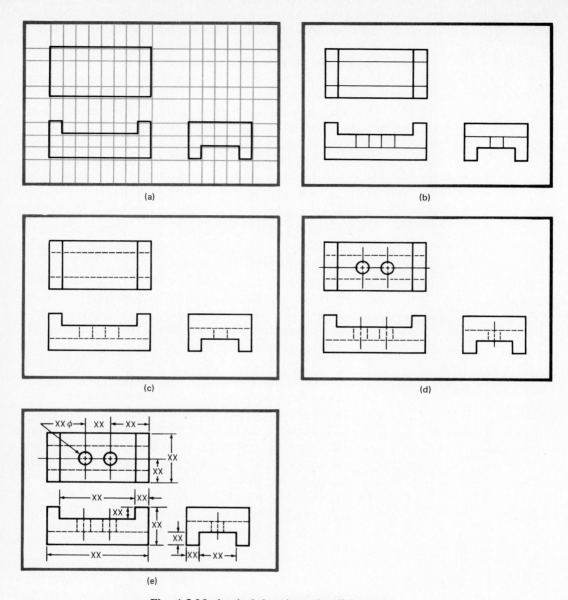

Fig. 4-5 Mechanical drawing using light pen.

method is that measuring, adding, and subtracting operations need not be performed by the user. The system can automatically calculate the length of each dimension prior to entry on the screen.

4-7
Symbol
Development
Using a
Joystick

It may not always be possible to obtain software containing all of the symbols unique to every application. In that event, it may be desirable to develop them from scratch. After development, the symbols can be stored for future recall. As with the other topics covered in this text, there is more than one way to develop a symbol. One method is to position the cursor on the screen by means of a joystick. After the positioning is done, lines and arcs are drawn to form the desired symbol. The procedure to accomplish symbol development follows.

1. Make sure the system is on and joystick is operational.
2. Some systems will display a square grid network on the screen. A sample grid is shown in Fig. 4-6(a). The size of the grid pattern is predetermined by the program. If the exact size of a symbol to be developed is important, the grid point placement can be changed. A smaller grid pattern can be used, and a computer programmer can make this alteration. If such a change does not yield sufficient accuracy, do not use a joystick. Exact coordinates may be keyed in using the alphanumeric. Even though lengthy, the alphanumeric procedure does produce maximum accuracy, if such accuracy is required.
3. Either buttons on a function board or keys on an alphanumeric may be used. The procedure outlined in Sec. 4-3 was illustrated with a function board. For diversity, the procedure outlined here will use the alphanumeric keyboard. Keys connected to the program are used to represent operations on the screen. A sample of keys and their meanings follows.

PROMPT KEY	OPERATION	MEANING
M	MOVE	This operation allows the cursor to be moved to a new position without drawing a line.
D	DRAW	This will draw a line from the last pointed location to the present position.
A	ARC or CIRCLE	This will draw an arc or circle with a specified radius.
L	LABEL	This operation allows alphanumeric entry.
E	END	This operation is used to terminate the drawing.

The user executes each operation by pressing the appropriate letter on the alphanumeric keyboard.

4. Use the joystick to position the cursor at the desired starting location for the symbol. The joystick is manipulated as described in Sec. 2-10.

5. Press key M on the alphanumeric. This signals the starting point for the symbol to be generated.

6. Use the joystick to position the cursor at the desired end location for the line segment.

7. Press key D on the alphanumeric. A line will be drawn from the first endpoint selected in Step 4 to the second endpoint selected in Step 6. This is illustrated in Fig. 4-6(b).

8. Repeat Steps 6 and 7 for the remaining straight line segments in the symbol. This is illustrated in Fig. 4-6(c).

9. If a circle is required, first locate the cursor at a position on the circle circumference. This is done by manipulating the joystick.

10. Press key A on the alphanumeric. Instructions will appear on the screen, such as: INCREMENT ANGLE, RADIUS, START ANGLE, END ANGLE.

11. An arc or circle may be generated by entering the instructed data using the keyboard—for example, 15, 0.125, 0, 360. With these instructions, a complete circle will be drawn having a 0.25 diameter and 15° straight line increments around the circumference. The complete symbol representing a globe valve is illustrated in Fig. 4-6(d).

12. You can generate other symbols on the screen by repeating Steps 4 through 11, as required. The screen may appear as shown in Fig. 4-6(e).

13. After each symbol has been generated, it may be permanently stored for future use. Some systems refer to this permanent filing as *library*. Library procedures will be covered in Chap. 5.

Summary

This chapter analyzed the development of basic engineering drawings using CAD equipment. Several variations were offered. The exact

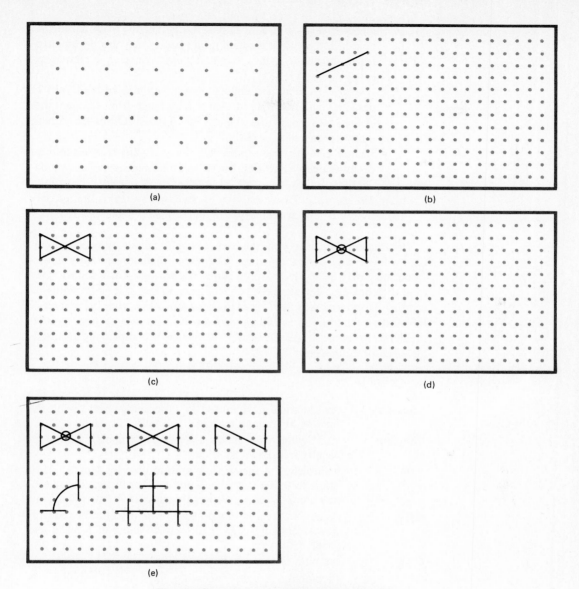

Fig. 4-6 Symbol development using a joystick.

style used by a design drafter will depend on many factors, including the following.

- *The type of equipment.* Mini systems will be likely to utilize a graphics tablet and function board or menu pad. An alternative to this is the use of a joystick or thumbwheel cursor control. Several larger systems use a light pen in conjunction with a function board. A few micro or small mini systems may use the alphanumeric keyboard with a function board. Several combinations exist.

- *The product line.* Depending on the product, certain types of drawings will be required. These may range from standard mechanical scale drawings to nonscale symbolic schematics. Again, many combinations exist.
- *Design and drafting experience.* As you gain experience, you discover many shortcuts. These will alter procedures as you develop drawings.
- *The software.* The capability of any CAD system is limited only by the extent of memory size and software sophistication.

This chapter has given you, the user, several methods by which to prepare a basic engineering drawing. After these methods are fully understood, they may be applied to more complex drawings. Once some degree of proficiency has been attained, you will begin to feel as if your traditional drafting experience was like "drawing on a stone slab with berry juice." Remember, the procedures will vary somewhat from manufacturer to manufacturer. Refer to the specific instruction manual accompanying a particular piece of equipment.

Terms to Know

Capacitor	An electrical device used to store energy and permit the flow of alternating current. Normally, designated C.
Diagram	A drawing made up of a series of symbols. These are usually not drawn to scale.
mm	Millimeter. A metric term used to describe length. *Milli* refers to 0.001 (one-thousandth). One thousand millimeters are in a meter. Approximately 25.4 mm equal 1 in.
Mylar	A durable, long lasting polyester film used for the preparation of drawings. *Mylar* is a trade name of Keuffel and Esser.
Ohm	An ohm is the unit of resistance.
pF	Picofarad. A unit of measure equal to 10^{-12} farads. A *farad* is the unit of capacitance.
PNP	Designation for the type of transistor known as *positive-negative-positive*.
Q	Designation for a transistor. A transistor is a semiconductor usually made of silicon. It causes changes in current and voltage.
R	Designation for a resistor. A resistor is an electrical device used to oppose the flow of current.

Schematic   The arrangement of symbols and manner in which they are connected on a diagram.

Symbol   An abbreviation; a code used to represent a component. Many national codes contain symbols. Once you learn the code, your ability to communicate ideas and information increases.

Problems

The following problems may be solved either with or without the use of CAD equipment. Simulations of an alphanumeric keyboard and a function board can be used. The answers will be expressed in chart form rather than on a CRT screen. Each grid square in the figures is 0.12 long. The X-Y zero axis is located at the lower left of each figure.

1. Keyboard Line Drawing. Use an alphanumeric keyboard to describe the process of straight-line drawing creation. Convert Fig. 4-7 into a word description. Write out the sequence for each step of the process. The X and Y coordinates for each line endpoint must be specified. Start at point A. Proceed sequentially around the part.

Prepare a chart of each endpoint location using the following format.

ENDPOINT	X COORDINATE	Y COORDINATE
Identify each endpoint line: e.g., A.	Location	Location

2. Function Board Line Drawing. Use a function board to describe the process of straight line drawing creation. Use the board shown in Fig. 4-1(a). Convert Fig. 4-7 into a word description. Write out the sequence for each step of the process. The X and Y coordinates for each line endpoint must be located. Start at point A. Proceed sequentially around the part. Each press of a cursor movement button will move the cursor 0.12 (the distance between one square grid).

Prepare the sequence using the following format.

LINE	PARTIAL PROCESS
Identify each line: e.g., AB.	Initial cursor location. Press MOVE program button. Press cursor movement button(s) ? times. Press LINE program button.

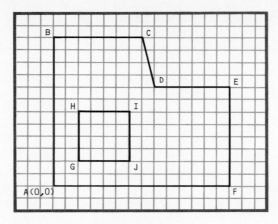

Fig. 4-7 Straight line drawing.

3. Function Board and Keyboard Arc Drawing. Use a function board and alphanumeric keyboard to describe the process of circle-arc drawing creation. Convert Fig. 4-8 into a word description. Write out the sequence for each arc of the process. The center, radius, and angle of arc must be indicated. Start at the center. Begin at the smallest arc and proceed outward.

Prepare a chart for each arc using the following format.

CIRCLE/ARC	PARTIAL PROCESS
Identify each circle or arc.	Locate the cursor. Press CIRCLE program button. Key in desired radius. Key in start angle. Key in end angle. Press End or Return key.

4. Function Board and Keyboard Shape Description. Describe the process to create the drawings assigned by your instructor. Write out the sequence for each line and arc. Use the format shown in Problems 2 and 3. Fig. 4-9 or drawings taken from a traditional drafting text may be used for this purpose. Convert each drawing into a word description. Combine the process used in Problems 2 and 3 for line and arc drawings. Additionally, create three views rather than a single view of the object.

5. Function Board and Keyboard Size Description. Describe the process to dimension the drawing created in Problem 2. Use a function key-

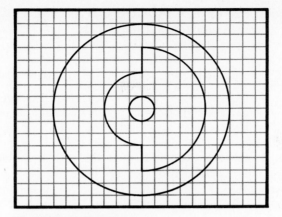

Fig. 4-8 Arc drawing.

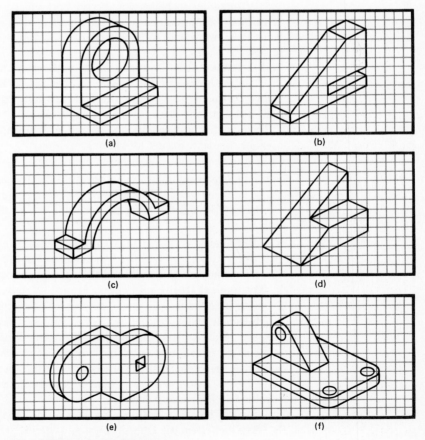

(a)

(b)

(c)

(d)

(e)

(f)

Fig. 4-9 Drawing assignments.

board with LINE, LEADER, and TEXT program buttons. Write out the sequence for each step of the process.

Use the following program buttons to place each function.

FUNCTION	FUNCTION BOARD BUTTON
Extension line.	Use LINE program button.
Dimension line.	Use LEADER program button.
Dimension.	Use TEXT program button.

6. Function Board and Keyboard Size Description. Describe the process to dimension drawings created in Problem 4. Use a function keyboard with LINE, LEADER, and TEXT program buttons. Write out the sequence for each step of the process.

Use the program buttons listed in Problem 5 to place each function.

The following problems may be solved by using menu selection. The menu may be considered as either a part of a graphics tablet or menu tablet. Answers will be expressed in chart form rather than on a CRT screen.

7. Mechanical Line Drawing Using a Menu. Use the menu shown in Fig. 3-4(a) to describe the process of mechanical line drawing creation. Convert a rough sketch into a finished drawing. Use Fig. 4-7 expressing both its shape and size.

To solve this problem, use the procedures outlined in the digitizing sections of this text, except as follows:

- Create a dimension by selecting the two endpoints and the DIM menu item. This will specify the complete dimension.
- Write out the sequence for each step of the process.

8. Mechanical Arc Drawing Using a Menu. Repeat Problem 7 using Fig. 4-8. Arcs may be created by selecting, in order, first arc endpoint, center, second arc endpoint, and the appropriate menu.

9. Mechanical Drawings Using a Menu. Use the menu shown in Fig. 3-4(a) to describe the process of mechanical drawing creation. Convert a rough sketch into a finished drawing. Any sketch may be used for this purpose. Sketches may also be taken from a traditional drafting text. Any number and selection of problems may be assigned by your instructor. To solve these problems, use the procedures outlined in the digitizing sections of this text. Also use the procedures for dimension and arc placement as specified in Problems 7 and 8.

Write out the sequence for each step of the process.

10. Piping Schematic Diagram Using a Menu. Use the menu shown in Fig. 4-4(a) to describe the process of schematic diagram creation. Convert a rough sketch into a finished schematic. Any sketch may be used for this purpose. Sketches may also be taken from a traditional drafting text. Any number and selection of problems may be assigned by your instructor.

To solve these problems, use the procedures outlined in Sec. 4-5. Write out the sequence for each step of the process.

11. Electrical Control Schematic Diagram Using a Menu. Repeat Problem 10 except switch to the menu shown in Fig. 4-4(e). Add start and stop momentary push-button switches to the menu selection.

The following problems may be solved by the methods using a light pen. Answers will be expressed in chart form rather than on a CRT.

12. Light Pen Line Drawing. Convert drawing Fig. 4-7 into a word description. This problem is similar to Problems 2 and 5, except use a light pen. Refer to Problems 2 and 7 for the format to use for shape and size description.

13. Light Pen Arc Drawing. Convert drawing Fig. 4-8 into a word description. This is similar to Problems 3 and 7, except use a light pen. Refer to Problems 3 and 6 for the format to use for shape and size description.

14. Light Pen Mechanical Drawing. Describe the process to create drawings using a light pen. Write out the sequence to describe each shape and size. Fig. 4-9 or drawings taken from a traditional drafting text may be used for this purpose. Any number selection of problems may be assigned by your instructor.

Note: The availability of CAD equipment will enhance solving the Chap. 4 problems. Solutions will be made directly on a CRT screen. This option will most certainly provide for a more interesting experience.

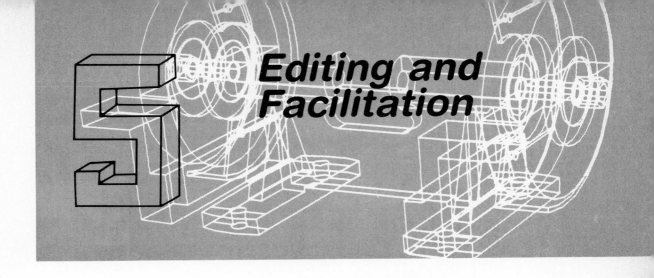

Editing and Facilitation

5-1 Introduction

After you develop the ability to create a basic engineering drawing, you may wish to study additional features used to facilitate the basic procedures. Functions that are common, but not necessarily required on every drawing, will be included. Generally, these will fall into the following categories.

- Revision or modifier methods.
- Preservation.
- Additional geometry generators.
- Miscellaneous commands.

A drawing in the process of being created forms on the screen an image with straight and curved lines. Because mistakes can be made, provisions to alter the image are needed. These alterations are referred to as *revisions*. Modification of a previously prepared drawing also falls into the revision category. A drawing that has been prepared and stored can, at any time, be recalled and readily modified. The modified drawing might be utilized for a completely different application. This is one of the real time-saving features of CAD.

There are several methods used to revise a drawing, depending on the software and the type of equipment. Some will remove only one line, while others remove the complete image. Various names given to some of the revision, or modifier, methods include:

- Erase.
- Delete.
- Redraw.
- Shift.
- Scale or size.

Once an engineering drawing or symbol has been completed, provisions to keep it should be available. It may be preserved on different media, depending on whether a micro, mini, or mainframe system is used. Preservation procedures include:

- Save to tape.
- Save to disk.
- File.
- Library.

Additional geometry generators beyond the basic ones covered in Chap. 3 exist. They are more involved than the basic application of two dimensional, multiview drawings prepared in Chap. 4. Methods include:

- Sectioning.
- Auxiliary view.
- Rotate or turn.
- Three-dimensional or isometric.

There are many special functions and commands found on various manufacturer equipment. This is especially true of mainframe systems and sophisticated mini systems. These functions and commands may vary significantly from system to system; therefore, an in-depth treatment is useful only for one particular manufacturer's equipment. Thus, special features will be treated with only a brief introduction.

5-2
Erase

The ERASE modifier, like an eraser on a chalkboard, is used to remove a complete image from the CRT screen. This is especially useful on storage tube terminals. The entire image may then be repainted on the screen. The erase function, however, is executed much more quickly than the erasing of a chalkboard. Also, removal is complete, with no trace of the image or erasure remaining. The procedure normally is easy to complete. Usually, just one press of the appropriate button will accomplish complete removal. The "big green flash" will occur. The button, whether on a function board or on an alphanumeric keyboard, will be given a name. On a function board it may be ERASE or ZAP. Some manufacturers use the term PAGE or HOME PAGE for keyboard identification. ERASE or ZAP may also be used to remove only a portion of the image.

5-3 Delete

The DELETE modifier is used to remove a point, a cursor movement, or a line. As previously mentioned, DELETE is also known by several other titles such as ZAP and ERASE. Depending on the system, different procedures may be used. A function board or a function board with a light pen are common equipment to use.

Function Board

Using a function board program button to delete a point, movement, or line requires that the button be appropriately indicated. It may be permanently marked on a board for use with larger systems. Other smaller systems might use menu switching on either a function board or menu pad. Interchangeable mask cards, which are placed over the buttons or pad, are used. A sample mask is shown in Fig. 2-13. These are changed with a software change. Consequently, the name given for DELETE may vary. It depends on who has developed the software. The term DELETE will be used in this section. The procedure includes the following steps.

1. The system must be in operation with an image on the screen. Suppose, for example, a line or symbol was added incorrectly to this image. Fig. 5-1(a) shows the inclusion of an incorrect line from a previous drawing, Fig. 4-1(g).
2. Press the DELETE button. The last *line* drawn will be removed from the screen as shown in Fig. 5-1(b).

An alternative DELETE procedure includes these steps.

1. Press the DELETE button. Instructions will appear on the screen. The instructions may ask how many lines or moves to delete.
2. Key in the appropriate number (i.e., 1, 2, 3, etc.) on the alphanumeric. Press End or Return. The number keyed in will instruct the removal of that many points, moves, or lines. If the number 3 were keyed in, for example, the previous three operations would be deleted.

Note: the order of removal is the reverse of the order drawn—last on, first off. Some programs have been developed to remove a portion of the image no matter when it was drawn. In this case, the cursor has to be positioned at the desired removal location before the DELETE button is pressed.

Light Pen

A light pen can be used to delete a point, a line, an arc, or a circle. Generally, any point or line can be removed regardless of when it was placed on the screen. For example, suppose both the last line and the first arc shown in Fig. 5-1(a) are incorrect. The procedure to remove both is as follows.

1. Select and press the appropriate program button on the function board. (One manufacturer uses the term SHOW.) When the button is pressed, a menu is displayed on the screen.
2. Use the light pen to select the appropriate menu item. Again, various names, such as DELETE and ERASE, may be used.
3. Use the light pen to select any point, line, arc, or circle. For example, point to the arc drawn in Fig. 5-1(a) with the light pen. Activate the pen. The arc will be removed as shown in Fig. 5-1(c).
4. Repeat Step 3 for any number of deletions. For example, point the light pen to the last line drawn in Fig. 5-1(a). Activate it. The result will appear as shown in Fig. 5-1(d).

Note: by using the light pen, you may remove any portion of an image from the screen. This is a distinct advantage over the func-

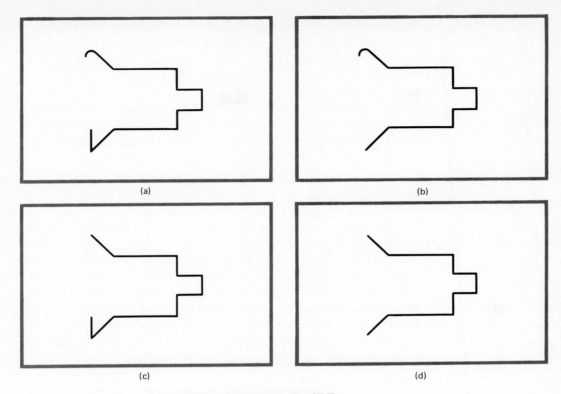

(a)　　　　　　　　　　　　　(b)

(c)　　　　　　　　　　　　　(d)

Fig. 5-1 Delete lines from the CRT.

tion board method. It does not matter when the image segment was drawn. Last on, first off has no significance.

5-4 Redraw

Some systems completely redraw the object each time a function is executed. Others do not. If your system does not, you may find it desirable to occasionally use a REDRAW function. This is especially true when excess points are on the screen as a result of a deletion, of a move, or of changing your mind after pressing a certain button. Redrawing the image will remove this clutter. Also, a redisplay will show you if the last execution was done satisfactorily. The simplest way to redraw is to use a system having a program button for that purpose. You simply press the REDRAW button on the function board, and the current image is completely redrawn. The redrawing occurs in the exact same sequence that the image was originally drawn in. This will aid the design drafter in remembering which line was drawn in what order.

5-5 Shift

SHIFT is also known as OFFSET or REPOSITION. It allows you to change the graphic position either of a portion of a drawing or of a complete drawing. You can accomplish this by using either a function board or both a function board and light pen.

Function Board

Do not confuse SHIFT with the shift key on the alphanumeric keyboard. The alphanumeric shift key is used to place uppercase characters on the screen. The SHIFT program button will move the image up, down, left, or right. This ability is often important during the preparation of a multiview drawing. For example, after one view has been drawn, it may become clear that there is not enough room for a subsequent view. The front view shown in Fig. 5-2(a) has been constructed too far to the center. It must be shifted to the left. The procedure to accomplish this is easy.

1. First, move the cursor to a position at the left of the last point displayed on the screen. This new position is shown by the cross hairs in Fig. 5-2(a). Move the cursor by pressing the cursor direction buttons described in Sec. 3-4, under "Function Board," and shown in Fig. 3-7. If a joystick is available, the cursor may be moved in the manner described in Sec. 2-10.
2. Press the SHIFT program button. The new image will be displaced by the amount of cursor movement. It will reappear on the screen in the position shown in Fig. 5-2(b).

The complete drawing can be shifted quickly and easily. It may be done as often as desired at the discretion of the user.

Light Pen

A light pen may be used in conjunction with a function board for an image shift. Portions of a drawing, rather than the complete object, may be moved. These portions include a line, an arc, a circle, or an

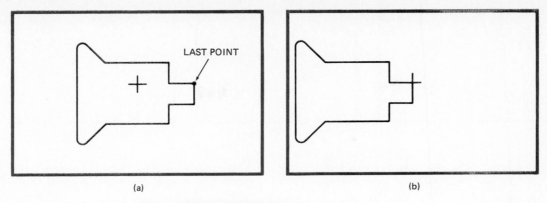

(a)   (b)

Fig. 5-2 Shifting an image.

irregular curve. Each segment may be duplicated at any distance from the original segment. This is a useful function for repositioning. This function also may be used for quick repeat of many identical segments at various locations. For example, you may wish to reproduce several identical parallel lines. Shift makes this possible.

A method used to shift a single line segment consists of the following steps.

1. The system must be in operation with an image on the screen. First, press the appropriate program button (e.g., SHIFT, OFFSET, or REPOSITION). Message instructions will appear on the screen.

2. Follow the instructions on the screen. Select the element to be duplicated with the light pen. Such an element is shown in Fig. 5-3(a).

3. Next, select the desired new position with the light pen. You can also accomplish this by using the alphanumeric to key in the desired offset location. The line will appear in duplicate as shown in Fig. 5-3(b).

The original line may be either left on or removed from the screen. If you wish to remove it, execute the DELETE procedure described in Sec. 5-3, under ''Light Pen.'' The screen will appear as shown in Fig. 5-3(c). This procedure may be repeated as often as desired. It may be used for any segment on the screen.

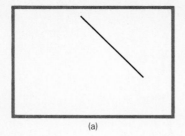 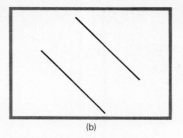 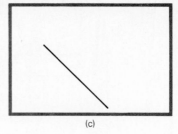

(a) (b) (c)

Fig. 5-3 Shifting a line segment.

5-6 Scale

The SCALE or SIZE function is used to change the size of the display. This function is useful if the drawing generated is somewhat large for the screen. Also, you can increase the scale ratio significantly to more clearly view small details. SCALE will change the size of the display, but it may or may not change the scale of the drawing. It does enlarge or reduce the overall drawing without changing scale. For example, it can be used to double the size of a display so that additional information may then be keyed in on the drawing using the original numeric values. The result will be the same drawing and text at the larger (e.g., double) size.

There are a variety of ways to change the scale. A drawing may be enlarged or reduced by means of a function board or a function board with a light pen. The alphanumeric keyboard is an important support device. It provides for an exact scale ratio change.

Function Board

The procedure to enlarge or reduce the display using the function board follows.

1. After an image has been created on the screen, move the cursor to the center. Do this using cursor direction buttons on the function board as shown in Fig. 3-7.
2. Depress the SCALE (or SIZE) program button. Instructions will appear on the screen. They will ask what scale ratio change is desired.
3. Using the alphanumeric, key in the desired ratio. For example, to double the drawing size, key in 2. Press End or Return. The entire drawing will be redisplayed twice as large. For a half-size drawing, key in 0.5, and

so on. First locate the cursor at the screen center if you wish the image to be redisplayed without a shift in position. Refer to Sec. 5-5 for the procedure used to shift position.

If you wish to see only a portion of the picture blown up, place the cursor central to it. A large-scale ratio may then be employed. Much of the object will fall outside the screen limits. Only the needed portion will be shown on the screen. One may have to experiment a bit by trying different ratios before obtaining the desired redisplay.

Light Pen

Light pen procedures will vary some depending on the software. Also, alphanumeric input may or may not be used. The common variations in the procedure are given here.

1. After the image has been created on the screen, press the appropriate program button. It may be a SCALE, SIZE, or WINDOW button. It also may be a button that will display on the screen a menu that includes SCALE or SIZE. Again, this depends on the software. If a menu is displayed, use the light pen to select the menu item. Next, instructions to proceed will appear on the screen.
2. The instructions will allow the use of either a light pen or the alphanumeric for the size change. One method using a light pen involves activating it on the screen in a certain position. For example, activating it above the center may decrease the size, below the center will increase the size. The higher it is activated, the greater the size reduction. Activating it lower reverses the effect. The major drawback to this method is that of accuracy. The exact size change will not be known. The change is, however, accomplished very rapidly. The alphanumeric may be used to key in the exact scale ratio. This may be accomplished as described in this section—Step 3 under ''Function Board.''

Using WINDOW, you can change the size of the entire display or of only a portion of the display. On some systems, the X and Y scale changes are independent. For example, suppose an object is drawn as shown in Fig. 5-4(a). It is possible to change the size in the X direction to one ratio and the size in the Y direction to another. For example, suppose you leave the window size in the X direction the same and double the size in the Y direction. This will result in an elongated object, as shown in Fig. 5-4(b).

Press the appropriate program button and follow the directions on the screen to accomplish window size changes.

Changing the window size of a portion of the display may require defining limits. The limits may be keyed in by coordinate values. This will form an imaginary box around that section to be resized. Again, the procedure involves pressing the appropriate program button and following the directions on the screen. To get an idea of the window concept, place yourself in a room and look out the window. You see a rectangular portion of the view. Now move closer to the window: you now see an enlarged, wider area. In general, window size changes are only temporary display modes. They are designed to enable you to view a large drawing on a small CRT. WINDOW should not be confused with SCALE. The latter is permanent for any particular drawing.

5-7
Save or File

An engineering drawing or symbol has been created on the screen. The question that now arises is, What should become of it? Very often, a significant amount of time has been invested. If the system should be turned off for any reason, all of the work put into the

Fig. 5-4 One direction window size change.

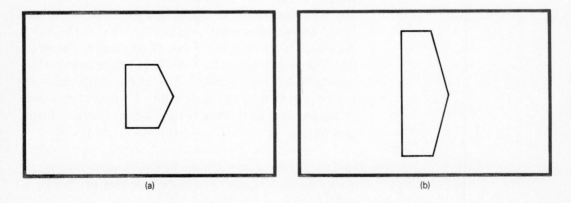

(a)

(b)

design or drawing development might be lost. The random access memory (RAM) discussed in Chap. 2 only provides for temporary storage. To prevent the loss of any drawings many systems automatically store work after a specific number of commands have been executed. Some work, however, is still occasionally lost. At any rate, after a drawing is created, you may want it on permanent record. If the drawing is not on permanent record, it cannot be reused after the shutdown of the system. For use at a future date, the entire drawing would have to be recreated, which would be a time-consuming needless process. The drawing may be stored on a permanent basis by its being transferred to a tape or disk. Larger systems will refer to this function as FILE. This way, a permanent record will exist, and the drawing can be recalled at any time. You may need, for example, to prepare a similar drawing with a few variations. The original drawing can be recalled. Next, revisions can be made rapidly, resulting in a new drawing. A copy can then be made. The new drawing also may be stored for future recall.

Saving a drawing on a tape or disk is common to micro and mini systems. Depending on length, several may be contained on one tape or disk. The ways to save or file include these methods.

Tape Storage

1. After the finished work is on the screen, insert a new tape. Refer to Sec. 2-5 for specifics. This tape must be premarked. It was done by saving a certain space for each drawing to be loaded on the tape. A string of messages must be typed in. Refer to the specific manufacturer user's manual for the exact premarking method.
2. Press a program button on the function board. It will be designated by a term such as SAVE TO TAPE. Instructions will appear asking for a file name and/or number.
3. Respond to the instruction by keying in the requested information. For example, it may be a number (e.g., 1) and the name of the part (e.g., shaft support).
4. Press End or Return. The data will be saved. It is stored in either binary or ASCII (American Standard Code for Information Interchange), depending on the type of commands used.
5. After the information is saved, the tape may be removed.

Tape Recall

Data which has been stored on a tape may be recalled at any time. The procedure involves the following.

1. Reinsert the tape.
2. Press a button to display the tape contents on the screen. The button may be DISPLAY FROM TAPE or AUTO-LOAD, among other descriptions. Instructions will appear asking for a file name and/or number.
3. Respond to the instructions by keying in the requested information.
4. Press End or Return. The stored drawing will be displayed on the screen. Before it can be displayed, however, it must first be found. Since tape cannot be accessed randomly, a sequential search is conducted. Just as with a recorder cassette, there is no way to break into the tape. The tape will begin at the beginning and progress through each program until the desired program is found.

The methods of tape storage and recall allow a drawing or symbol to be utilized over and over again. Tapes, however, are not widely used on CAD systems. A disk is by far the preferred storage medium for mini systems.

Disk File Generation

A file of drawings may be permanently stored on a disk. There are two basic file forms—sequential and random. Information which is entered sequentially starts at the first empty space. It works towards the end of the allocated space. The first empty space may be either at the beginning or just past the last data entered.

Disks may also be random-filed, which means that information may be retrieved or entered at any location. The disk is analogous to a phonograph record. You can listen to the first melody on the album. You also have the ability to immediately switch to any other song by moving the needle. This alternative is not available with a tape. Random filing is also referred to as *direct access*. A random file must be divided in two or more sections. The size and number of these sections must be specified. They may be as small as 1 byte. Once the data has been recorded, however, it is not normally added to. New information will completely replace existing information in the section.

To file information for the first time, a blank disk must first be initialized or formatted. A procedure similar to the following may be used.

1. Turn on the power switches. Insert a blank disk into the drive cavity. Refer to Fig. 2-14. Be sure the write-protect hole is not covered. Push the disk as far as it will go or until you hear a click. Close the door cover.
2. Start a file using the appropriate alphanumeric command. This may require typing in such information as INIT HELLO, CREATE, or INIT. Refer to the manufacturer user's manual for the specific command.
3. Press End or Return.
4. Type in a string of messages (refer to the user's manual) in order to specify name, length, number of sections, and whether sequential or random form is required. Random access is common for a disk.

The file will now be created and an invisible pointer is automatically positioned at the beginning.

Disk Storage

1. After the finished work is on the screen, it may be stored. Use the initialized disk described in this section under "Disk File Generation."
2. Press the appropriate button. It will be designated by a term such as SAVE, SAVE TO DISK, or FILE. Instructions will appear on the screen.
3. Respond to the instructions by keying in the requested information. Normally, this will include typing in the part number and/or name. For example, it may be the name of the part (e.g., shaft support).
4. Press End or Return. The drawing will be filed on the disk. Storage may be either binary or ASCII.

After storage, the disk may be removed. Some mini systems use more than one disk drive. This makes it possible to file a drawing without removing another disk containing the programs. If only one drive is available, it must be used for both purposes. The first disk containing the programs is inserted. Its contents are loaded into RAM before the second disk is used.

Disk Recall

Data stored on a disk may be reinserted for use at any time. The procedure involves the following.

1. Reinsert the disk into the drive capacity. Type in the necessary information and press End or Return.
2. Press the appropriate program button, which may be referred to by a term such as DISPLAY FROM DISK, FILE, CALL, or RECALL. Instructions will appear asking for the file name and/or number.
3. Respond to the instructions by keying in the requested information.
4. Press End or Return. The stored drawing will be immediately displayed on the screen.

Mainframe File and Recall

Large systems will generate a file of drawings. Such a procedure entails the following.

1. After the finished work is on the screen, press the FILE program button. An instruction message will appear on the screen.
2. Follow the instructions on the screen. Normally, the part number, and/or file name will have to be keyed in using the alphanumeric.
3. Press the appropriate alphanumeric key or program button. The drawing will be filed.

As in tape and disk storage, the drawing is recalled at any time. This may be done by the following procedure.

1. Press a CALL or RECALL program button. Some systems use the FILE program button and a light pen to select a CALL or RECALL menu item. In either case, a

listing of the filed drawings will appear on the screen.

2. Normally, the part number and/or file name will have to be keyed in by means of the alphanumeric.

3. Press the appropriate alphanumeric key or program button for the redisplay.

SAVE and RECALL allow a drawing or symbol to be used over and over, a significant time-saving feature that makes CAD much more efficient than conventional drafting. Rather than being started from scratch each time, a drawing may be recalled and added to. For example, a company may have requirements for drawings that are quite similar. Common features can be prepared as an incomplete drawing and stored. Each recall will require only the addition of information unique for that drawing. This way, engineering drawings are rapidly and cleanly produced. Traditional means of accomplishing this involve procuring a translucent sepia copy of the original. The copy is then revised to reflect the alterations. This method requires time and often results in a messy appearance. Also, the type of medium used is not durable, thus the new drawing has a short life span.

Overlay drafting is another traditional method used for many years. It involves laying vellum or Mylar on top of the original. The desired portion of the drawing can then be traced. This is quicker than preparing the drawing from scratch. It is, however, much more time-consuming than using CAD. The speed at which drawings can be revised using CAD is a major advantage over conventional drafting and may be reason enough to warrant the financial outlay for equipment.

Another feature of SAVE and RECALL is that data can be readily transferred from system to system. A rough cut of a design can be made using a small system. The information can be "dumped" on a disk and later transferred to a larger system. This alleviates the continuous tying up of a large system. Various system transfers include any information from a tape or disk to:

- Another disk.
- Another tape.
- CRT screen.
- Mainframe storage.
- Manufacturing processes such as numerical control or robotics.

5-8
Library

A library may consist of many files, depending on the system. For example, it may be large enough for all system contents. On the other hand, it may be small enough to be restricted to a particular user. A library can be used to store drawings, or it may contain commonly used symbols and details. A library example is shown in Fig. 5-5.

A library that is made up of symbols on file may be used for schematic drawing creation. This is a modified version of the schematic preparation of Sec. 4-3. The procedure consists of these steps.

1. A standard library must first be in existence. It may be developed in several ways. Refer to Sec. 4-7 for a method of preparing symbols using a joystick.

2. Next, the system must be in operation. Press the appropriate program button. The button may directly call LIBRARY. If not, the second step of selecting the LIBRARY item from a menu is necessary. A light pen is a common piece of equipment used to accomplish this. In either case, instructions will appear on the screen to request the file number from the library and the symbol or detail number from the file.

Fig. 5-5 Library versus file.

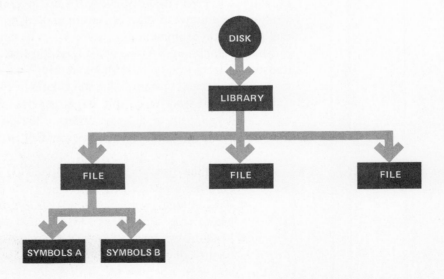

3. Enter the file and detail numbers with the alphanumeric keyboard. Press the appropriate button or key. The library item will be displayed on the screen.

5-9 Sectioning

Before studying procedures to section a drawing on the CRT screen using CAD, you must understand the topic of conventional sectioning techniques. With this understanding, the importance of a sectioning feature is clear. Sectioning is particularly important for any part or assembly having a complicated interior. The portion of the detail represented by material at an imaginary cutting plane must be crosshatched. The sectioning procedure involves placement of the cross-hatching. Different methods of accomplishing this are available. Again, it depends on the equipment used. The common methods include using a function board or a function board in conjunction with a light pen. A procedure for the latter of these is given here.

1. Create an outline describing the boundaries of the object to be crosshatched.
2. Press the appropriate program button on the function board. A menu will appear on the screen.
3. Use the light pen to select the XHATCH (crosshatch) menu item. Instructions will appear on the screen. A +45° and −45° incline is the most common cross-hatching orientation. The prompts will most likely suggest standard incline first. Other inclines can be drawn so as not to parallel object lines.
4. Indicate that the direction is satisfactory or key in a different value. If other information is not keyed in, the system may draw the section lining at 45°. Many systems will automatically execute the most common feature. This is referred to as *default*. The sectioned object will appear on the screen.

5-10 Auxiliary View

An auxiliary view may be created without the use of a special program. Just as a right side view is created by the design drafter, so is the auxiliary. In fact, a right side view is an auxiliary view shown in a normal position. If the depth dimension is known, the auxiliary view is constructed using the basic geometry generators described in Chap. 3.

Large systems contain an AUXILIARY VIEW function. It provides the design drafter with the capability of developing other views necessary to complete the shape description. A program button on a function board is included for this purpose. If a light pen is used, a menu having a variety of choices will be available. The procedure involves several sets of instructions. These will vary depending on each parameter and the type of equipment used. Because of the many variations, a common procedure cannot be outlined. Refer to the manufacturer's user manual.

5-11 Rotate

A two-dimensional rotation command may include turning the entire object, a portion of the object, or just one line segment. The segment may include either a straight line, a circle, an arc, or an ellipse. An example of a program used for rotation was illustrated in Sec. 3-5, under "Function Board and Alphanumeric Input." The part of the instruction to accomplish this was the TILT instruction. The table in Sec. 3-5 shows that for (c) a desired rotation angle of 45° was keyed in. The segment, in this case an ellipse, was displayed on the screen. It was rotated 45° counterclockwise from the horizontal as shown in Fig. 3-12(c). Other procedures are included below.

Function Board

This procedure is followed to rotate a figure using a function board.

1. First, prepare the object on the screen. An example is shown in Fig. 5-6(a).
2. Press the ROTATE program button. Instructions will appear on the screen asking for the rotation angle.
3. Key in the desired angle in degrees using the alphanumeric. Normally, the rotation will occur in the counterclockwise direction. A 45° rotation and a 225° rotation will produce reverse images.
4. Press End or Return. If 45 was entered, the rotation will appear as shown in Fig. 5-6(b). The result of entering 225 is shown in Fig. 5-6(c).

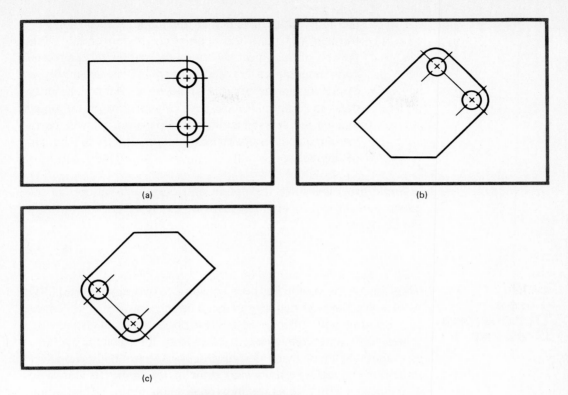

Fig. 5-6 Rotating an object.

Function Board and Light Pen

An object or portion of an object can be rotated using a light pen in conjunction with a function board. The previous procedure detailed complete object revolution. A procedure to rotate only a portion of the object is given.

1. Prepare an object on the screen.
2. If a group function is available, group that portion of the drawing to be rotated.
3. Next, use the light pen for the menu display. Select the item TURN or ROTATE and activate the pen. Instructions will appear on the screen asking for the rotation angle.
4. The angle may be identified either by using the light pen or by keying in the value. If accuracy is not an important consideration, use the light pen. Just position the pen in

the approximate location of the angle of turn. Activate the pen and press the appropriate button or key. The portion of the object shown on the screen will be rotated correspondingly. Greater accuracy may be accomplished by keying in the number of degrees. After data entry, press the End or Return key. The portion of the object will be redisplayed in a rotated position. It will be rotated in a counterclockwise direction, exactly that number of degrees.

Some programs have the option of clockwise rotation. In that event, a negative (−) sign may have to be entered prior to the number of degrees.

5-12 Three-Dimensional Drawing

Thus far, all discussion has been confined to two-dimensional (2-D) work. For the vast majority of engineering drawing applications, 2-D drafting will suffice. Multiview projection, which uses two dimensions to describe three, is considered the standard operating procedure (SOP) of many design offices. Occasionally, however, three-dimensional (*axonometric*) drawing capability is desirable. This is especially true as the individual gains more sophistication. The user may, for example, be required to prepare isometric spool drawings for a process piping application. This can be accomplished, on a limited basis, using a basic system. Lines, for example, may be drawn inclined both to the right or left at 30° from the horizontal. These, with a vertical line, establish the three major axes of an isometric drawing as shown in Fig. 5-7(a). Likewise, an ellipse or partial ellipse may be drawn tilted and used to represent an isometric circle or isometric arc. The method used to perform this, however, is cumbersome and requires a considerable time expenditure. The use of a rather extensive software package enables isometrics to be drawn quickly. If this capability is a necessity, the extra expense for the software will be a sound investment.

One method used to prepare a three-dimensional view follows.

1. First, draw two views of a part as shown in Fig. 5-7(b). Use conventional CAD methods as described in Chaps. 3 and 4.
2. Press the appropriate program button. A menu will appear on the screen.

3. Use the light pen to select the 3-DIMENSION function. Instructions will appear on the screen.
4. Draw a line at the specified angle, shown in Fig. 5-7(c) as line 1.
5. Start a third view in any convenient location, in this case the lower right. Use line 1 as the line of sight. Draw a new line 1 in the third view at the same angle.
6. Construct a second line (2) from the vertex of the new line 1 (in the new view). Draw it to a specified length and at a specified angle with respect to the horizontal line 3, as shown in Fig. 5-7(d).
7. Start another view at any convenient location, in this case the upper right. Use line 2 as a line of sight, similar to that of Step 5. Establish a point for the origin (X = 0, Y = 0) in this view.
8. Use the appropriate program button or menu item for construction of the isometric. The result is shown in Fig. 5-7(e). Variations of this procedure exist. For example, it may be possible to rotate the view or erase some of the previously drawn construction lines; depending on the software composition.

Three-dimensional (3-D) capability is common to the large mainframe system. Also, many of the mini turnkey units have this capability. A system designed for 3-D geometric data base gives the user an added powerful tool. Moving away from 2-D and into 3-D design enhances system performance. Designs may now include dynamic capability, rotational capability, and modeling. A drawing on the screen, for example, can be rotated in space about either the X, Y, or Z axis. The modeling features include wire frame, surface, and solid bodies as shown in Fig. 5-8. Obviously, these features give a CAD unit very powerful design capability.

5-13 Miscellaneous Modifiers

Many specialized CAD features exist, and each manufacturer has variations unique to its system. Since so many exist, it is not possible to outline every procedure for different systems. Consequently, only one illustrative miscellaneous modifier example will be given. The selection is CORNER. It is found on the CADAM system. It consists of a method to trim two elements (lines) to their mutual intersection and may be used to shorten either straight or curved

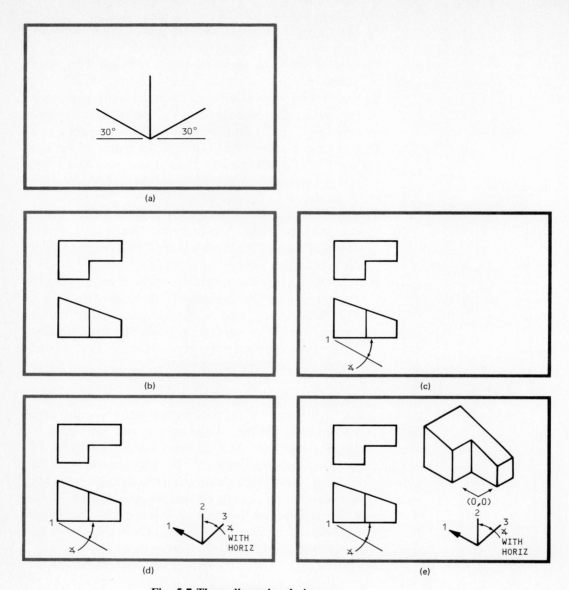

Fig. 5-7 Three-dimensional view.

lines of unlimited length. The method entails the following steps.

    1. Various elements must first be displayed on the screen as shown in Fig. 5-9(a).

    2. Press the CORNER program button. The message SEL ELEM (select element) is displayed.

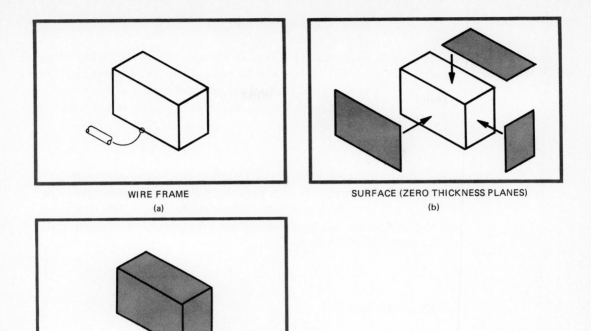

WIRE FRAME
(a)

SURFACE (ZERO THICKNESS PLANES)
(b)

SOLID
(c)

Fig. 5-8 Three-dimensional modeling.

3. The user selects one of the two elements to be cornered using a light pen. For example, choose the horizontal line. The message changes to read IND END SAVED/ SEL ELEM 2 (indicate end of line to save/select element 2).

4. It is possible to produce incorrect results under certain conditions. To preclude this, indicate the end to be saved. Activate the light pen at the location shown in Fig. 5-9(b) by an X. Next, select the second element (the vertical line). The following message instructions and menu will then be displayed:

IND END SAVED/KEY RAD = (   )

TRIM ALL/TRIM @ 1/TRIM @ 2/NO TRIM/CON-VEX/CONCAVE

5. Selection of the TRIM ALL menu item results in the

modification (shortening) of both selected elements as shown in Fig. 5-9(c).

6. If a rounded corner is desired, key in the radius of the corner. Next, use the light pen to indicate the direction of the round (toward the center of the arc). The elements will be modified and displayed on the screen as shown in Fig. 5-9(d).

The above procedure has been abbreviated. Only the highlights have been covered. It does give you a good idea, however, of the very specific and detailed data that must be input. Since so many special features are in existence, this example was outlined to serve as a typical illustration.

Fig. 5-9 Cornering.

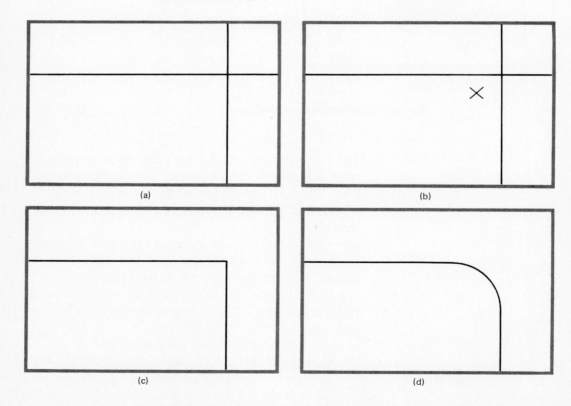

5-14
Bill of
Material

A drawing may be generated by applying the various procedures outlined in this text. After completion, it may be desirable to specify material size. This may be accomplished either automatically or manually. The automatic option may be available through the use of additional software. Some programs are capable of sizing individual parts, while others complete assemblies. If the prepared drawing is of one part, it may be easily determined. The overall size of a sheet metal pattern layout will be displayed, for example, by the press of the right button.

A bill of material for an assembly drawing can be created by using symbolic representation. Symbols are used which correspond to the identities of certain parts. The symbol may represent any component. It may range from a piping elbow, to a PNP transistor, to a particular type of bolt. Each symbol will uniquely identify particular parts. It will serve to "flag" it on the drawing. Counting the number of times it appears will determine the quantity of that item. This may be accomplished by "dumping" information from the unit on to another unit. It may be transferred, for example, to a printout. This transfer process is referred to as *off loading*. When the printout encounters a symbol, it will be counted. The count will continue until completion. The total quantity can then be specified with the part name, number, and/or size. This will constitute a line item of a bill of material table.

Automatic bill of material generation may become complicated with a mainframe system. This is especially true for a large organization having many CAD employees. The problem arises that once a symbol has been selected, it must be maintained as such. This means it always must represent the same part and size identity. With so many employees using the same system, keeping this standardization may become difficult. A dedicated system, however, many not encounter the same problem since control is localized.

Summary

This chapter dealt with many additional procedures involved in CAD drafting. The ones covered are common to all areas of design and drafting. While not required for every engineering drawing, they are crucial to high productivity. For example, if a drawing cannot be saved after it has been created, all development time is lost.

As should be apparent by now, each procedure will vary somewhat by manufacturer. The ultimate goal of each, however, is the same, that is, the creation of usable drawings. The most common ways to accomplish this include:

- *Function board.* A function board may be built in as part of the terminal. More likely, however, it is a separate unit. The function board, or function keyboard, contains several program buttons. These are used to call up a function, a command, or the object of a command. A variation to the function board is a menu pad or menu tablet. Buttons are not pressed. The program or menu item is selected with a puck or stylus.
- *Function board and light pen.* This combination of equipment may be found on large systems. It involves both the use of instructions (called message options or prompts) and a menu selection. They are displayed on a CRT screen. The work is conducted in response to these instructions.
- *Graphics tablet.* A graphics tablet will normally have a menu on the surface. The surface area of the tablet is used to digitize. Sketches (or other rough work) are placed on the tablet. During conversion from a rough sketch to the screen, the lines are straightened. The drawing will appear in finished form on the screen. Tablets contain a menu selection. The menu may be located at the top, at the bottom, or at either side of the tablet. It also may contain any type or number of symbols.

Remember, the examples given, while common, are only illustrative. They will vary somewhat from unit to unit. Thus, consult the manufacturer's user's manual for exact instructions.

Terms to Know

Axonometric
A graphical representation that expresses three faces of an object. The faces are inclined to the plane of projection. The length, height, and depth are shown but not in perspective.

Cross-hatching
Section lining indicating that the surface has been cut. Section lines usually consist of inclined, thin parallel lines. If there are different line patterns, they will indicate different materials. ANSI now uses cast iron hatching for all materials.

Intersection	The point at which two lines meet. For example, the crossing of two center lines is the intersection that defines the center of a circle.
Isometric	A view showing three visible faces of a cube that appear equal in shape and size. The side faces are at an angle of 30° to the horizontal.
Medium	A drawing material that can normally be reproduced. Vellum and Mylar (thin plastic film) are the most popular.
Process piping	A category of design and drafting falling within the giant field of industrial plant design.
Scale ratio	The number which indicates how much larger or smaller the shape of an object is shown. For example, a 2 means that a drawing shows an object twice as large as actual.
Sepia	A translucent medium. If a translucent reproduction is made from an original, the reproduction also becomes reproducible.
Spool drawing	A three-dimensional isometric schematic diagram of a portion of a piping project.
Surface	Like a two-dimensional plane. It is an area having a thickness considered for practical purposes to be zero.
Three-dimensional view	A view of an object expressing its length, height, and depth. Also called 3-D.
Translucent	Light can pass through. With reference to drafting media, the use of translucent material for drawings allows for reproducible prints.
Window	A visual display screen divided into one or more sections.
Wire frame	A series of thin wires connected to form a three-dimensional object.

Questions

1. What do the editing and facilitation features add to an engineering drawing?
2. What are the advantages of being able to revise a CRT graphic display?
3. What is one of the primary time-saving features of CAD over conventional drafting?
4. What is the advantage of DELETE over ERASE?
5. What is the advantage of deleting using a light pen rather than a function board?
6. What type of CRT must repaint the entire image during a DELETE function?

7. Name an important feature of REDRAW.
8. Why would you want to shift an image on the screen?
9. What procedure is used to clearly view a small detail on the screen?
10. How can a drawing the size of a football field be displayed on the CRT?
11. What is the popular way to save a drawing after it has been generated on a minisystem?
12. What are the advantages of three-dimensional drafting?
13. What are the most common ways to create a CAD-generated drawing?

Problems

1. Function Keyboard Line Removal. Write out the process to delete two lines that have been mistakenly placed on a drawing. Use the second method presented in Sec. 5-3, under "Function Board."

2. Function Keyboard Disk Storage. A drawing has been prepared. After it is completed, you want to have a permanent record of it. Write out the process to permanently save the drawing on a floppy disk.

3. Function Keyboard Drawing Rotation. After a drawing has been prepared, it must be rotated. Write out a process to rotate it using the method presented in Sec. 5-11, under "Function Board."

Manufacturers' Equipment

6-1 Introduction

Now that the fundamental knowledge of CAD is understood, how will it be applied? What type of equipment will you be likely to encounter? As mentioned throughout the first five chapters, a multitude of systems, software, and options are available. No single system has captured the market. There is no one brand name that describes CAD. Because of this, it may not be possible to determine which system you will be working with. Even if you are presently working on one type of system, there is no guarantee that you will continue to do so. The company, for example, may upgrade equipment, or you may change jobs. Thus, a broad-based knowledge common to all systems becomes essential. Such a knowledge may quite readily be adaptable to a multitude of systems.

This chapter will acquaint you with a broad cross section of what is available by showing you manufacturers' literature for selected systems. If you need to know about other computer equipment, books that deal solely with specific manufacturer equipment descriptions are available. The manufacturer product range in this chapter includes producers of:

- Software.
- Individual components of CAD systems.
- Small- and medium-sized turnkey systems.
- Large mainframe units.
- Systems for drafting and those for design.

Included here are photographs and brief write-ups supplied by each manufacturer for its equipment. These manufacturers have been found to be enthusiastic and willing to supply data. Included here are photographs and a brief write-up describing the features and capability of the equipment. Where to write or call for further information is also included. Upon request, each manufacturer will gladly supply this information.

Many design and drafting offices have been equipped for years with systems similar to those outlined in this chapter. Some firms have advanced so much that traditional design and drafting offices seem to be a generation behind by comparison. To remain competitive, it is virtually mandatory that everyone involved in engineering design and drafting utilize the tools of CAD.

6-2 Checklist for a New System

There is a lot of basic information you must acquire when encountering an unfamiliar CAD system. The following checklist will help you to get acquainted.

1. *What type of system is it?* Is it a micro, mini, or mainframe system? This will tell you a lot regarding the capability that can be expected.
2. *What is the capacity?* If possible, determine the system size. For example, is it 16K bytes or 1 megabyte?
3. *What type of peripheral equipment is available?* How will data entry be made? Will it be with a program function keyboard (function board), graphics tablet, joystick, or light pen?
4. *Locate the manufacturer's user manual.* This will be an indispensable guide to specific procedures.
5. *Locate all power switches.* Is the complete system activated by one switch or must each piece (micro and mini) be turned on separately?
6. *How is the system driven?* For micro and mini systems, are floppy disks, hard disks, or tapes used? How is the software inserted? For mainframe, software insertion is usually not a concern.
7. *What is the start or log-on procedure?* How is a new drawing started? How do you call up an existing stored drawing?

8. *Although the keyboard is standard, are additional buttons or keys located on the terminal?* What is their purpose? Are they used as a function keyboard? Some terminals, for example, have extra numeric keys to provide quicker number entry.

After basic information has been acquired, you will be prepared to work with the system. Initial data entry can begin. Refer to the methods from the appropriate sections in Chap. 3. The sections utilized will depend on the available input equipment.

**6-3
Alphabetical
Listing of
Selected
CAD Manu-
facturers**

- Adage, Inc.
- Apple Computer, Inc.
- Auto-trol Technology Corporation
- Bausch & Lomb Inc.
- Bruning Company
- CADAM, Inc.
- California Computer Products, Inc.
- Calma Company
- Cascade Graphics Development
- Computervision Corporation
- Control Data Corp.
- Evans & Sutherland Computer Corp.
- Gerber Systems Technology, Inc.
- Hewlett-Packard Company
- Information Displays, Inc.
- Intergraph Corp.
- ISSCO Graphics
- Koh-I-Noor Rapidograph, Inc.
- Lexidata Corporation
- McDonnell Douglas Automation Co.
- ManTech International Corporation
- Matrix Instruments Inc.
- Megatek Corporation
- Perkin-Elmer Corporation
- Prime Computer, Inc.

- Sperry Univac
- Summagraphics Corporation
- T & W Systems, Inc.
- Tektronix, Inc.
- Terak Corporation
- Vector Automation, Inc.
- Versatec Co.

Adage, Inc.,
One Fortune Drive
Billerica, MA 01821
(617) 667-7070

Three-dimensional, high-performance graphics for mainframe users

Full three-dimensional, high-resolution displays
Direction connection to mainframe channel of
IBM, or IBM-compatible, computer
Compatible with NCAD$_{TM}$ software
Maximizes off-loading of host computer
Connection to microwave, telephone "T1,"
56 Kbaud, or fiber optic links

The Adage 4370 Work Station is a high-performance, high-resolution, full three-dimensional vector refresh display. Designed to attach directly to the mainframe channel of IBM, or IBM-compatible, computers, the 4370 permits the local display, modification, and manipulation of complex, highly structured images. Working with software packages such as Northrop's three-dimensional NCAD System or CADAM®, the 4370 simplifies the most

demanding design challenges. Several firmware options allow the user to exploit fully the 4370's advanced capabilities.

A network of high-speed microprocessors reduces channel-program execution time, handles interrupts quickly, and speeds up user interaction with complex images.

In addition to improved display capabilities and advanced ergonomics, Adage 4370 Work Stations can be flexibly placed in relation to the mainframe. The 4370 can be located up to 3 mi (4,827 m) from the mainframe channel via coaxial-cable pairs or remotely via microwave, Bell System "T1," fiber optic, or 56 Kbaud links. Maximum range for full-duplex transmission rates is 3 Mbaud up to 1.5 mi (2,414 m) or 1.5 Mbaud up to 3 mi (4,827 m). A full-duplex transmission rate of 56 Kbaud is also available.

Optional features that add to the 4370 Work

Station's flexibility include: local zoom, hardware window, data tablet, variable control dials, joystick, and local hard copy.

4370 Hardware

The 4370 consists of a Channel Unit, a Control Station, and up to three Display Stations. Each control station and display station incorporates a high-resolution vector refresh CRT display monitor.

The Channel Unit (CU/4201) connects directly to the mainframe channel of an IBM, or IBM-compatible, computer and provides data transmission for up to four clusters of displays. Each cluster can include up to four displays, for a total of 16 displays on one IBM-channel connection.

The Control Station (CS/4370) contains the display controller, which incorporates two microprogrammed processors. One processor controls interrupts and communications with the Channel Unit. The second processor, called a Digital Graphics Controller, contains three-dimensional and optional two-dimensional firmware that: (1) fetches and interprets data from the refresh buffer, (2) performs all image manipulation, and (3) handles all interactive peripheral devices.

The controller also contains a Refresh Buffer Memory and High-Speed Stroke Generator. The memory stores host-generated images and system parameters. The stroke generator converts digital data to analog signals to drive up to four displays. Interfacing for interactive peripheral devices is also located in the controller.

Three Display Stations (DS/4370) can be added to a CS/4370 control station, for a total of four displays in a 4370 cluster. Displays can be separated by up to 190 ft (58 m) per 4370 cluster. Each display station is physically identical to the CS/4370, except that DS/4370s do not contain a display controller.

Display Monitors are mounted on a large work surface that accommodates the standard interactive devices (Light Pen, Alphanumeric Keyboard, and Programmable Function Keys), as well as the optional Digital Data Tablet, Joystick, and Variable Control Dials.

Apple Computer, Inc.
10260 Bandley Drive
Cupertino, CA 95014
(408) 996-1010

Apple computers represent the widest combination of price and performance in the mid to upper range of the personal computer industry. Its systems range in complexity from an easy-to-learn machine for dedicated applications to one that can fulfill the word processing and bookkeeping needs of a small company.

There are two basic models in Apple's family of computers. Both models include high-resolution color and black and white graphics capability, the BASIC, FORTRAN, PASCAL, and PILOT languages, interfaces for supporting peripheral devices, and a wide variety of applications programs.

Apple III

It is a fully integrated computer system with a built-in 143K byte disk drive, up to 256K bytes of main memory, a human-engineered, 74-key keyboard with a 13-key numeric keypad, built-in disk controller for handling up to four floppy disk drives, new Sophisticated Operating System (SOS 1.1) software, and an improved central processing unit. Available now for the Apple III is ProFile, a complete mass-storage

unit featuring an intelligent controller, a 5¼-in Winchester technology disk drive, a power supply, an interface card and driver software.

Major advances over the earlier Apple II include an 80-column upper- and lower-case display, more main memory and a higher capability operating system, a built-in disk drive, improved multicolor capability, and 16 shades of gray for vivid graphics presentations in black and white.

The applications packages are:

- Business Graphics III
- VisiCalc™ III
- Apple Writer III
- Business BASIC
- Apple III PASCAL
- Access III
- Script III
- Mail List Manager

By simply changing program disks, the user can tailor the Apple III to perform a wide variety of data manipulation and word processing assignments. Apple III also has an emulation mode in which it can run Apple II software—thus protecting the software investment of Apple II owners.

Auto-trol Technology Corporation

Auto-trol Technology Corporation
12500 North Washington Street
Denver, CO 80233
(303) 452-4919

Auto-trol Technology Corporation, a leading manufacturer of computer-aided design/computer-aided manufacturing (CAD/CAM) systems, announces the availability of the Advanced Graphics Workstation (AGW).

The AGW is a low-cost 32-bit stand-alone CAD/CAM system. AGWs can be linked together to form a high-speed, local area network with distributed processing. In addition, the network can be connected to a host processor such as Digital Equipment Corporation's VAX series of computers. All of the configurations use Auto-trol's 32-bit architecture/engineering/construction and mechanical design and manufacturing software.

More than just an intelligent workstation, the Advanced Graphics Workstation provides a dedicated computer for every user. Each AGW uses its own 32-bit processor manufactured by Apollo Computer, Inc., of Chelmsford, Massachusetts. Because of the AGW's low cost, it is now cost-effective for a company to give every engineer, designer, or drafter an individual 32-bit CAD/CAM system, while still allowing it to be a part of a corporate network.

The AGW, therefore, represents significant innovations in the CAD/CAM industry. It is the first turnkey CAD/CAM system that offers the speed, power, and capacity of 32-bit processing at a low cost. Also it is the first CAD/CAM system that can provide high-performance local area networks of dedicated computers in a distributed environment. And because each workstation has its own computer, it is the first system to eliminate the problem of performance degradation as work stations are added. Performance is level whether the network consists of two AGWs or one hundred.

The advanced local area networking architecture employs 12 million bits per second baseband transmission. This supports fast transfer and retrieval of data, and effective sharing of resources on the network. Thus, through Auto-trol's Advanced Graphics Network (AGN) each user has available the performance and capabilities equivalent to those of large 32-bit mainframes. In addition, the Advanced Graphics Workstation's hierarchical communications capabilities allow interfaces to large mainframes such as Digital Equipment, IBM, and Sperry Univac computers.

Auto-trol and Apollo have entered into a joint marketing and development agreement in support of Auto-trol high-performance workstations.

BAUSCH & LOMB ▼

Bausch & Lomb Inc.
1212 East Anderson Lane
Austin, TX 78752
(512) 837-8952

The Producer Drafting System is a turnkey system with three work stations where drafters can work concurrently.

At the Interactive Station, drafters see their drawings as they create them. They can scale the drawing, rotate it, zoom in to look at or add detail, merge drawings and subdrawings, and easily revise them.

At the Plotter Station, high-quality originals can be drawn at very high speeds in a variety of line weights and colors. The drafter can choose whether to use ballpoint pen or india ink on paper, vellum, or mylar. And every copy is of camera-ready quality.

At the electronic drawing board or digitizer, the drafter can take existing drawings or rough sketches and quickly enter them into the system where they can be stored, revised, or plotted.

An extensive drafting library, which contains thousands of commonly used symbols and figures, over a dozen lettering styles, and 25-plus crosshatch patterns, is a standard feature of the Producer Drafting System.

Because of the Producer's ability to create, modify, and store drafted material, it has applications in many fields. Firms producing architectural, electrical, or mechanical drawings have already found that the Producer greatly increases productivity and reduces turn-around time, while improving the quality of the finished drawings.

Bruning Company
1800 Bruning Drive West
Itasca, IL 60143
(312) 351-7550

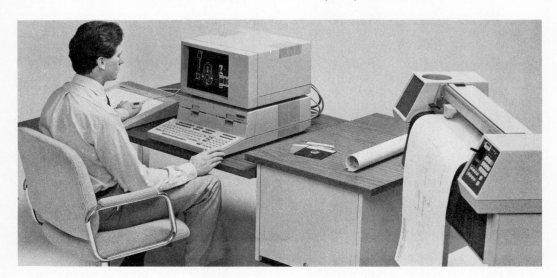

The Bruning Company's Easy Draf[2] CAD system can:

- Draw construction lines.
- Draw real lines.
- Draw arcs.
- Specify the scale factor of the picture.
- Calculate exact distances.
- Erase any part or all of a line, arc, or geometric shape without redrawing the picture.
- Add straight line or arc pointers to the picture with diamond, hexagon, octagon, or balloon terminators.
- Label drawings using letters and/or numbers.
- Do cross-hatching.
- Check the dimensions of a picture—in feet and inches, decimal, or metric format—and change them as required.
- Rotate the picture to any orientation.

- Save the picture for later use, or whatever part has been drawn, by recording it on a floppy disk.
- Retrieve and use any picture (or parts of pictures) stored on disks, such as shapes or symbols of bolts, gears, doors, or electrical elements. The size can be changed.
- Make a mirror image of a picture for faster creations of designs that are symmetrical about one or more axes.
- Detect errors by matching up the parts of a picture that must fit together.
- Draw and display components separately and then combine them into a whole assembly.
- Create clean, new drawings from parts of existing drawings with or without modifications.
- Achieve exact registration.

CADAM ®

IBM Corporation
900 King Street
Rye, NY 10573
(914) 934-4000

Lockheed-California Company
2660 W. Empire Avenue
Burbank, CA 91504
(213) 847-3400

Adage, Inc.
One Fortune Drive
Billerica, MA 01821
(617) 667-7070

The Computer-Graphics Augmented Design and Manufacturing System, known as CADAM®, is a high-function, general purpose design drafting package containing analytical and conceptual design aids for use by engineers in 3-D conceptual design, design drafting, N/C part programming, finite element modeling, and other engineering or manufacturing applications.

Functionally the CADAM software may be divided into an interactive, or real-time portion, and a batch portion. The interactive portion allows a console operator to construct geometry to be stored in a large data base. This geometry may later be input to batch routines to produce hardcopy on virtually any plotting device

®CADAM is a registered trademark of CADAM, Inc.

currently available, or to produce data to run digitally driven devices such as numerical control and wire wrap machines or flame cutters. Batch routines perform required data management functions on the data base. Additionally, batch routines are available to access the CADAM data base.

Both two- and three-dimensional shapes may be represented, using construction and development techniques familiar to the conventionally trained drafter. Lines, circles, ellipses, and curves are rapidly created under the direct control of the user. A matrix transformation feature assists the drafter in the development of oblique, isometric, and perspective views from existing views.

Design models may be retrieved immediately from the data base. Individual views may be stacked, juxtaposed, separated, or otherwise located within the arbitrarily defined drawing perimeter. Interfacing components, subassemblies, or drawing details may be shown simultaneously to assure compatibility. Conversely an assembly can be broken down into separate details to develop exploded views. Sizes and dimensions may be changed rapidly. Error-detecting logic reduces the incidence of human configuration errors. Precision to at least six digits is obtainable.

CADAM software is designed to assist the N/C programmer in developing a sequence of operations directing a specific machine tool to produce a part. The N/C part programming capability utilizes the displayed geometry of the part as the reference for creating the N/C program. Using the geometry already in the data base, a direct, accurate, analytical solution to the required tool path can be obtained. Program checking is facilitated by dynamic motion (animation) in the display to represent the tool path. The tool centerline data, as graphically displayed, may be selectively modified.

The CADAM system can operate either on a central mainframe computer supporting over 100 terminals or in a standalone or distributed mode using smaller processors. In the distributed or standalone configuration, an independent self-sufficient processor is located at the user's site. These processors can be networked to a central CPU that provides data management functions and communicates with each user's site.

The data link between processors is only used to pass data base information. It is not necessary for any interactive information to be communicated. Therefore, a low-speed line is sufficient to perform this task. The benefits of distributed processing are efficient management of a large data base, as well as the accessibility and propagation of smaller amounts of geometry to a large user community.

California Computer Products, Inc.
3320 East La Palma Avenue
Anaheim, CA 92806
(714) 632-0400

How the CalComp System Works

Workstations

This is where the operator "draws." The system supports multiple workstations. There are two CRT monitors in a workstation. One is alphanumeric and the other is graphic.

Workstation Monitors

The alphanumeric monitor gives the operator information requested via the keyboard, such as program status, lists of symbols available for use in drawing, and so on. It also prompts performance of necessary operations, step by step, and notifies an inappropriate choice.

The graphics monitor displays the drawing. It utilizes raster technology and the CalComp picture processor.

Picture Controller

With the picture controller (joystick), you can view the entire drawing or zoom in so close that a small object fills the screen. The zoom magnification ratio is 1000 to 1 or greater.

Keyboard and Tablet (Digitizer)

Drawing on the monitor is accomplished electronically via the workstation keyboard, tablet, and stylus.

As the stylus is moved lightly over the surface of the tablet, a "target" (called a cursor) moves correspondingly on the graphics monitor.

The Picture Processor The workstation contains the CalComp picture processor, consisting of seven individual microprocessors and memory.

System Processing Facility The system processing facility consists of three data handling components: CalComp's minicomputer, a CalComp-designed disk system, and a high-speed magnetic tape system.

The System Operator's Console A separate TTY System Operator's Console is dedicated to system commands, including plotting and programming operations. It can optionally be replaced by an alphanumeric monitor and keyboard.

Pen to Paper—The End Product Output options for the IGS-500 include a full range of CalComp ink-on-paper and microfilm plotters, as well as graphics printers.

Calma Company
5155 Old Ironsides
Santa Clara, CA 95050
(408) 727-0121

CHIPS (Integrated Circuit Design System)

CHIPS is an advanced, minicomputer-based, interactive graphics system for very large scale integrated circuit (VLSI) design work.

This turnkey system is based upon the industry standard GDS II data base management sytem. It features 32 bit precision to support VLSI work, color graphics terminals for designers, and software aids to enhance design implementation. Additional advantages include background processing for analysis programs and output formatting and application capabilities to tailor the system to the specific needs of the user. CHIPS is a total system applicable to all areas of graphic IC development.

DIMENSION III (Architecture, Engineering, and Construction)

This is an interactive computer graphics system for the architectural, engineering, and construction (AEC) fields. DIMENSION III is a practical and comprehensive automation tool which performs complex design, drafting, and engineering tasks.

With DIMENSION III, a designer works directly at a video display terminal to create three-dimensional designs of process plants, offshore structures, power plants, and other large construction projects. Designs become part of a data base from which material reports and other documentation can be derived.

The system boasts major advances for the architecture, engineering, and construction industry. DIMENSION III offers the most advanced three-dimensional piping and structural steel applications, as well as process and instrumentation diagrams (P&ID's), electrical schematics, equipment arrangement, steel detailing civil site preparation, and general mapping software for the AEC industry.

CARDS (Printed Circuit Design)

CARDS is a comprehensive computer-based interactive system for the design and production of printed circuits. The system encompasses all aspects of PC design and production from digitizing a schematic through final documentation and artwork, including features that handle net list generation; packaging, placement, and routing; automated design review; and NC drill and photoplot output.

STICKS (Symbolic IC Design)

STICKS is a dynamic, symbolic IC design system which allows designers to use symbols far less complex than actual circuit elements when laying out ICs. STICKS uses an auto-matic spacing system to lay out the circuit in as small a space as design rules allow. This leaves the designer free to concentrate on the more creative aspects of chip design. STICKS produces error-free designs in one-tenth the time previously required.

DDM (Design, Drafting, and Manufacturing System)

Introduced in 1977 and now an industry leader, DDM is a powerful, minicomputer-based system for three-dimensional computer-aided design, drafting, and manufacturing. This high-speed, flexible system enables a designer to explore several solutions to the design problem, perform engineering analysis, check clearances of moving parts, and produce engineering drawings and documentation including the preparation of NC tapes. With Calma's DDM/Solids software, engineers can see their designs as solid images, rather than "wireframe" representations. DDM systems provide design and manufacturing firms with greatly increased throughput, accuracy and control of the product cycle from initial design concept through manufacture.

CASCADE GRAPHICS DEVELOPMENT

**Cascade Graphics
Development**
1000 South Grand Avenue
Santa Ana, CA 92705
(714) 558-3316

CASCADE II (Microcomputer-Based Computer-Aided Drafting)

Cascade II is a low-cost multistation computer-aided drafting system that can be used to meet CAD training requirements or, in its more sophisticated form, the needs of an architectural or engineering firm. The **Cascade II** hardware and software system provides general purpose 2-D computer-aided drafting facilities applicable to architectural, electrical, mechanical, and process engineering operations.

The Software

The **Cascade II** has user-friendly software specially designed for 2-D graphics. The operator can use the menu-driven drawing tasks to create fundamental primitives such as lines, arcs, text, and combinations of these (groups). Symbols can be created or chosen from available symbol libraries which enable quick input of electronic and electrical schematic diagrams, P&ID's, architectural and structural-steel drawings. The operator can pan across or up and down the displayed drawing and zoom in to enlarge any specified drawing "window" or area. Both scaled and unscaled drawings can be produced in either English or metric units.

The **Cascade II** has an automatic dimensioning task, cross-hatching task, and other special graphics tasks.

Programs for high-resolution monochromatic and color displays, and architectural engineering applications are in progress.

Hardware Configuration

The **Cascade II** configuration is built on an Apple IIE computer disk system with 80K RAM, a special CGD-supplied tablet, an ASCII keyboard, and other options. Two configurations are possible. The **Cascade II** station can be used as a stand-alone or connected through a network to a central fixed-disk that can support up to eight workstations and 20 MB of storage.

The **Cascade II** displays a drawing with a 280 × 192 resolution on a 12 in diagonal screen. A graphics tablet provides an 11 in × 11 in digitizing area that can be used to select desired graphics tasks or input and edit displayed objects.

Since the basic hardware is not altered, other programs that are designed for Apple II computers can be interfaced to a plotter and/or a dot matrix impact printer.

A partial list of **Cascade II** functions follows:

Points
Text
Lines
Arcs
Flow lines
Move
Copy
Delete
Rotate
Scale (up or down)
Mirror
Copy repeat
Line widen

Line edit
   Move vertex
   Insert vertex
   Remove vertex
   Extend line
   Reference line
   Move segment
   Erase segment
   Gap line
   Unerase segment
Alignment
Create groups
Group library edit
Group edit
Digitizer setup
Menu setup
Crosshatch
Drawing defaults
   Scale drawings to any scale
   Set grids to any value
   Up to 255 levels
Text edit
Dimensioning (English or metric)
Zoom in
Pan drawing
Fast plot
Diagnostics
Drawing management
Easy edit
   Change pen number
   Change level number
   Change intensity
   Change kind
Property associating
Report generating

Any program written for the Apple II Plus can be used on the **Cascade II** including:

Business accounting
Educational programs
Business modeling/planning
Word processing
Inventory control
Engineering
Lab measurement/control

COMPUTERVISION

Computervision Corporation
201 Burlington Road
Bedford, MA 01730
(617) 275-1800

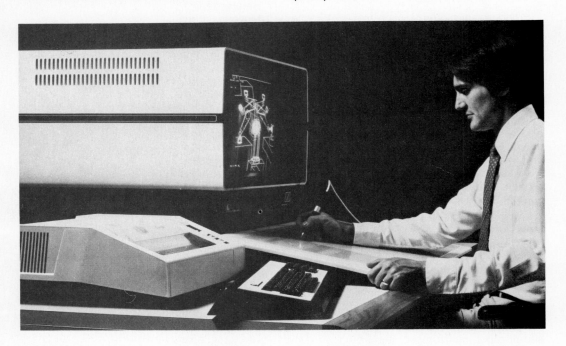

Employing CADDS® 4, Computervision's most sophisticated multiapplication software, Designer V offers the fastest response and the most extensive graphics capabilities of any Computervision CAD/CAM system. Designer V hardware and CADDS 4 software offer three-dimensional design capabilities and dynamics, through which the system greatly facilitates interaction with complex designs.

 CONTROL DATA

Control Data Corp.
8100 34th Avenue South
Minneapolis, MN 55440
(612) 853-2622

Finite Element Modeling

Control Data's UNISTRUC II system is an interactive graphics program that generates finite element models for structural analysis—from a terminal or directly from data generated by our design/drafting system. From data preparation to engineering drawings and reports, the system automates the tedious tasks usually encountered in structural analysis.

You generate a mesh—in Cartesian, cylindrical, or spherical coordinates—and rotate, section or view it from different angles. You can isolate elements of the model for viewing so errors can be identified and corrected before processing. And, after visually and analytically checking the model, you can use one of the major finite element programs for analysis. After analysis, results such as stresses and displacements are graphically displayed and reviewed through the system post-processor. The system can build models of up to 20,000 nodes, with larger projects analyzed by segmenting the model into blocks.

Graphics

The Terminal Independent Graphics System (TIGS) and the Universal Plotting Interface System (UNIPLOT™) provide complete control of your graphics environment.

The Terminal Independent Graphics System is a general software system that supports a variety of interactive graphics terminals. Because it allows the application to have a device-independent graphics interface, you can select and use the terminals that will help you solve your problems most efficiently.

The Universal Plotting Interface System creates files for plotting on almost any graphics output device. Input is received from the design and drafting process and then used to generate output in many forms, including check prints, final drawings, or release material.

Use Geometric Modeling, Analysis, and Automated Drafting to Speed Design

Control Data's computer-aided design system is based on industry-established, engineering-oriented application programs. The system includes programs for design, geometric modeling, analysis, and automated drafting.

Numerical Control Speeds Production

The numerical control segment of CD/2000 allows you to generate control tapes directly from your design geometry. Time is reduced to minutes rather than days or weeks—even for the most complex surfaces.

EVANS & SUTHERLAND

**Evans & Sutherland
Computer Corp.**
580 Arapeen Drive
Salt Lake City, UT 84108
(801) 582-5847

PS 300

The PS 300 is a self-contained, high perform-ance, interactive computer graphics system for the creation, manipulation, and modification of complex 2-D and 3-D data structures. The system is designed to handle many of the functions which normally reside in a host com-puter, such as memory management, building and modifying data structures, and interpreta-tion of interactive commands. The unique ar-chitecture of the PS 300 allows for the addi-tion of many optional accessories.

Features Distributed interactive graphics capability

Local high-speed interaction regardless of con-nection to host; no communication of irrele-vant information to host

Programmable local interaction of devices with graphic data structure

Complex graphical tasks may be completed locally due to power and flexibility of system

Parametric and rational parametric curve spec-ifications

B-spline and rational B-spline curve specifica-tions

User definable line patterns

Hierarchical picking capability, virtually unlim-ited object names

Terminal emulation capability

Optional Interactive Devices
- Data Tablet
- Alphanumeric Keyboard
- Control Dials
- 32 Lighted Function Buttons

Other Optional Enhancements
- Hardcopy Interface
- CSM Color Display
- PS 300/DEC DMR11-AE Interface
- Memory Expansion up to 4 Megabytes

Gerber Systems Technology, Inc.
40 Gerber Road East
South Windsor, CT 06074
(203) 644-2581

Basic System

Central Processing Unit
- Hewlett-Packard Series 1000 minicomputer
- HP-IB Bus for multiple device interface
- 512K byte High Performance Memory
- Additional 512K bytes of memory available

Sytem Software
- Easy to use data management system features English commands and tutorial user interface.
- Powerful file classification, listing, and re-trieval capabilities allow efficient data storage and retrieval.
- Foreground/background processing increases productivity.
- Dynamic file management facilitates handling of very large numbers of rapidly changing files.

Optional Hardware

Plotters
- Model 5131 Drafting Plotter for ANSI A

through D (ISO A4 through A1) size drawings
- Model 5132 Graphics Plotter for ANSI A (ISO A4) size drawings

Model 5181 Graphics Printer
- 120 character per second text printing
- Also provides for screen graphics hard copy
- 8½ in × 11 in fan-fold thermal paper

Model 5151 Free Cursor Digitizer
- 36 in × 48 in free cursor digitizer provides for easy entry of existing drawings into system
- Optional backlighting

Model 5161 Data Entry Tablet
- 11 in × 11 in surface for easy symbol selection
- Portable and adjustable

Disk/Cartridge Unit
- 27M byte Winchester-type fixed disk for high reliability and rapid access
- 64M byte disk available for large capacity on-line storage
- Integrated "streamer" cartridge for fast, full-disk backup (up to 64M byte) to a single tape

Graphic Workstation
- Easy-to-use pushbutton function keyboard and desktop cursor control arm
- Attractive, modular design fits comfortably into office or plant
- Separate graphics and message displays

- 19 in black-and-white raster display with 512 × 640 resolution
- Optional high resolution (1280 × 1024) raster
- 48 in wide wood-grain desk with optional 60 in wide extension and 90° wedge
- Separate, roll-around electronics module for easy access

Model 5051 Magnetic Tape
- Switch selectable 800/1600 bpi 9-track magnetic tape
- Provides transportation medium with industry standard interface

Paper Tape
- For N/C applications, 75 character per second punch and 300 character per second reader
- Available as punch only (Model 5172) or reader/punch combination (Model 5171)

Communications
The Model 5205 Gerber Network Module (GNM-1) Communications Controller allows Autograph to communicate with a wide range of systems using the following protocols:
- IBM 2780 Protocol permits communications:
  . . . Autograph to Autograph
  . . . Autograph to IDS-80
  . . . Autograph to Mainframe
- Direct Numerical Control (DNC) Links allow on-line part machining for many machine tools.
- Asynchronous terminal emulator allows Autograph to function as a terminal to most mini- and mainframe computers.

HEWLETT PACKARD

Hewlett-Packard Company
1501 Page Mill Road
Palo Alto, CA 94304
(415) 857-1501

Engineering graphics design problems can be resolved with a one-vendor software package from Hewlett-Packard Company.

Three modules, compatible with the HP 9845 family of desktop computer systems, offer general drawing, PC board layout, and schematic drawing capabilities.

Created for electronic circuit and printed-circuit board designers, HP Engineering Graphics System/45 (EGS/45) helps them increase individual production—saving up to 50 percent of the required PCB design and drafting time compared to manual methods.

EGS/45 is a key element in Hewlett-Packard's developing concept of a manufacturer's productivity network, a network that eventually will be able to communicate among all major departments of a manufacturing plant.

The new EGS/45 software product is available either as a complete package or as individual modules: a general drawing core, a schematic drawing module, or a PC board layout module.

General Drawing Core

With this module, the designer can create engineering drawings with primitive elements—lines, circles, rectangles, polygons, arcs, and text via user-definable screen menus. Groups of primitives can be named, added to the menu, and stored on mass media as recallable library parts. These parts then can be scaled, rotated, or mirrored when being added to a subsequent drawing.

The primitive elements and library parts are viewed on the CRT's drawing area. This drawing area can be thought of as containing up to 256 overlapping transparent layers, each containing a matrix of 900 million grid points that align the drawing elements. To meet the resolution required by the drawing, the user can select the number of grid points.

Screen editing commands allow copying, repeating, or moving objects on the CRT screen, as well as stretching lines, zooming, panning, and other time-saving functions. With other commands, the designer can specify line width, selectively displaying or plotting layers and grouping sets of parts for storage and reuse.

Some general drawing core applications include producing overhead slides, schedules, floor plans, and simple mechanical drawings. This core is required to use the other modules. The other modules include a PC Board Layout Module and schematic (electronic, piping, etc.) drawing module.

Information Displays, Inc.
28 Kaysal Court
Armonk, NY 10504
(914) 273-5755

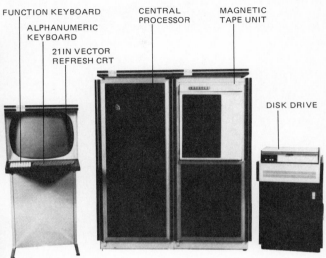

FUNCTION KEYBOARD

ALPHANUMERIC KEYBOARD

21IN VECTOR REFRESH CRT

CENTRAL PROCESSOR

MAGNETIC TAPE UNIT

DISK DRIVE

A turnkey computer-aided design and drafting system offering high-quality graphics displays, the IDI System 150 can significantly increase productivity and efficiency in any design/drafting or technical publications department.

Designed for a variety of uses, the IDI System 150 is an important tool for small, as well as large architectural, engineering, and construction firms. The system has been used to design everything from oil rigs to pistachio nut processing plants. Unusual applications include furniture design and bottle modeling. The IDI system is also unique in that in addition to its use as a drafting tool, it is a valuable technical publications production system.

IDRAW, the system's software packge, minimizes the training required for operation of the system and enables personnel to work in the everyday language of their individual specialties. Communication with IDRAW is accomplished by choosing from simple commands which appear and change on the display screen for each drawing operation selected.

These "menu" items provide quick access and continuous guidance throughout drawing creation.

In place of pen and paper, the designer, illustrator, drafter, or engineer is equipped with a light pen and works directly on a display screen (CRT). The system thus becomes a natural extension of the user's traditional work environment, with repetitious tasks performed in vastly quicker ways.

Without altering elements that need not be changed, the operator DYNAMICALLY moves, positions, rotates, deletes, or scales objects on the screen both rapidly and accurately. All actions are seen on the screen as they occur.

To complement IDRAW, IDI offers a cover-to-cover book composition and make-up package. ICAPS (Integrated Composition and Production Software) allows the merging of illustrations, tables, etc. created on the System 150 with text supplied from almost any source. In addition to integrating footnotes and legal boilerplate, ICAPS performs automatic (dictionary) hyphenation; numbers heads, subheads, and captions; vertically and horizontally justifies pages; unites widows and orphans; forces major sections to begin on odd-numbered (recto) pages; and extracts, sorts, and formats front and reference matter.

The IDI System 150's basic hardware can be augmented with options, including all major manufacturer's pen and electrostatic plotters, COM units, digital CRT phototypesetters, and digitizers. Applications specialties include Technical Publications, Architectural Engineering, Facilities Planning and Management, and General Drafting, while support services include installation, training, maintenance, and a software update service.

Intergraph Corp.
One Madison Industrial Park
Huntsville, AL 35807
(205) 772-2000

The System

For several important reasons, Intergraph has always incorporated proven design and drafting techniques when laying the groundwork for its automated approach.

The use of both menus and user commands linked with user-friendly tutorial routines is central to the productivity achievable in the Intergraph workstation design environment. Design and drafting operations associated with Intergraph software packages are quickly accessed and executed using the system cursor and accompanying menus, i.e., sets of symbols and commands linked with specific packages. Functions not on the menu are accessed as user commands each of which prompts the user every step of the way.

Although every Intergraph system is configured according to user requirements, a typical hardware configuration includes a central processor, one or more graphics workstations, a control console, on-line and archival storage subsystems, and output devices such as plotters and printers. To complete the system, Intergraph adds its software for graphics and nongraphics (textual) data creation and management, the requisite applications software and, when desired, third-party software.

Central to the Intergraph advantage is the choice of systems communications options. Workstations can communicate via cable link with the central processor over distances of approximately 6000 feet (2 km), and with remote processors at unlimited distances using modems and telecommunications facilities.

The Hardware

Intergraph tailors its systems to the individual user's specific needs, building in the potential for expansion as additional capabilities become desirable.

ISSCO Graphics
Sorrento Valley Boulevard
San Diego, CA 92121
(619) 452-0170

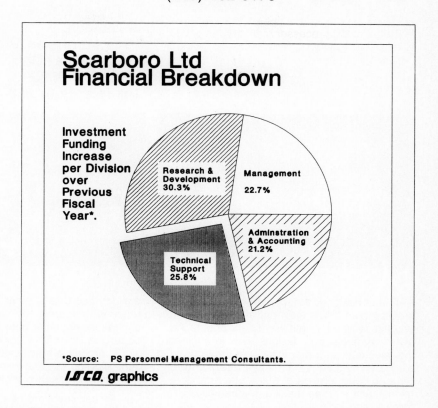

Simplicity—TELL-A-GRAF's language is conversational English, and it is being used daily by people with no knowledge of computers, as well as by experienced programmers.

Versatility—TELL-A-GRAF runs on a variety of computers and outputs to any graphic CRT or plotting device.

Reliability—TELL-A-GRAF's comprehensive software support includes on-site installation and education, automatic updates, complete documentation, PIHOTline service and problem analysis.

Koh-I-Noor Rapidograph, Inc.
100 North Street
Bloomsbury, NJ 08804
(201) 479-4124
Toll free (800) 631-7646
In Canada:
1815 Meyerside Drive
Mississauga, Ont. L5T 1B4
(416) 671-0696
Toll free (800) 268-4961

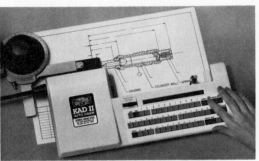

KAD II is designed for use directly on the drawing board. It is electronically controlled to produce a virtually limitless library of lettering styles, symbols, and designs used in engineering, electronics, and architectural drawings. It is also used to draw symbols and designs for drawings and formats of many other disciplines such as map making, mathematics, fluidics, and logic.

KAD II is a microprocessor-based system utilizing today's most advanced technology to letter and draw with liquid ink on most drawing surfaces. KAD II consists of three electronic components: The PLOTTER, which is connected to the CONTROLLER; and preprogrammed standard or custom ELECTRONIC TEMPLATE MODULES (ETM's), which are inserted one at a time into the Controller and activated by the Plotter keyboard.

PLOTTER
The Plotter weighs less than four pounds and can be attached to almost every type of drafting machine or used independently. It is completely portable and is easily carried from one drawing board to another. No special skills are required to operate KAD II after an initial demonstration. Any staff personnel of a drafting department can fill in nomenclature, dimensions, repetitive messages, and other information, allowing the drafter or designer to spend more time at creative drawing.

The Plotter keyboard has 12 function keys, plus 39 dual-entry character keys which can provide a standard "A" through "Z" sequential arrangement of many styles of alphabet letters, numerals, and symbols. Other letter arrangements can be specified for upper and lower case letters or other shift entries, providing a total of 78 characters. The keyboard can be preprogramed to identify and draw symbols and designs alone, or in conjunction with lettering styles. The choices are virtually unlimited and completely adaptable to individual requirements.

Visual proofing of keyboard entries before any actual ink plotting is made possible by a 32-character LED (Light Emitting Diode) red-light display with a 5×7 dot matrix.

LEXIDATA CORPORATION

Lexidata Corporation
755 Middlesex Turnpike
Billerica, MA 01865
(617) 663-8550

Lexidata Corporation's Model 8400/D is a high performance disk-based graphics workstation that supports multiple configurations of black-and-white or color graphics in either medium (640 × 512) or high (1280 × 1024) resolutions. This standalone product incorporates a powerful raster graphics subsystem, a 16/32-bit microprocessor with up to 1.75MB or RAM and mass storage systems in the form of a high performance, high capacity Winchester disk and a tape cartridge unit.

Lexidata offers the Bell Labs UNIX™ Operating System for the Model 8400/D product line. In addition, C, FORTRAN, and Pascal compilers are available, as well as a sophisticated full-screen editor for high-level program development. A key feature of this package is the Lexidata-developed library of graphics subroutines that can be used with C or FORTRAN application programs. This library substantially reduces the effort required to develop sophisticated graphics applications on the 8400/D workstation.

Included in the display processor subsystem is an Extended Graphics Operating System (EGOS), which handles the following functions: drawing vectors, circles, and polygons of varying line width and pattern; polygon fill; lookup table manipulation; blink, pan/zoom control; random or sequential pixel read and write.

Several graphics input devices are also available for the workstation, including data tablets, joysticks and trackballs.

Lexidata Corporation markets a variety of medium-to-high resolution display systems used in interactive computer graphics and imaging, principally aimed at the CAD/CAM, graphic arts, satellite, and medical imaging markets.

**McDonnell Douglas
Automation Co. (MCAUTO)**
P.O. Box 516
St. Louis, MO 63166
(314) 232-6443

UNIGRAPHICS is a standalone minicomputer-based turnkey system—no computer-programming expertise is required to use it. The system is unique in its machine-independence; it runs on several models of standard off-the-shelf minicomputers.

UNIGRAPHICS Functions

- **Geometry—**
The curves available in UNIGRAPHICS are lines, arcs, conics, and splines. Each of these curves can be constructed by a variety of methods; for example, there are 14 basic techniques for constructing a line.

- **Transformation and Editing—**
These functions allow portions of UNIGRAPHICS models to be duplicated, moved, or modified in various ways. For example, a block of text may be relocated, two curves may be trimmed at their intersection point, or the shape of a spline may be changed by moving a defining point.

- **Verification and Analysis—**
The user may verify the defining data of any UNIGRAPHICS entity, such as the center and radius of a circle. The analysis function allows the calculation of such various physical properties as the areas of planar regions or the weights of certain 3-D objects.

- **Patterns—**
  If a particular symbol, component, or subassembly is used repeatedly, it can be created as a UNIGRAPHICS "pattern." This pattern is named, stored on the system, and then can be inserted into any UNIGRAPHICS part simply by typing its name.

- **Dimensioning and Drafting—**
  UNIGRAPHICS provides semi-automatic methods for posting many different types of dimensions and tolerances in a variety of formats. In addition, text and labels may be created, and regions can be automatically cross-hatched.

- **Display—**
  These functions allow the user to examine the appearance of the model from any viewpoint and to "zoom in" on areas of special interest. Several different images of the model can be displayed on the screen at one time, displaying different views at various scales.

- **File Management—**
  This function allows the user to manipulate the various files the system generates.

**ManTech International
Corporation**
107 Ridgely Avenue
Annapolis, MD 21401
(301) 268-9010

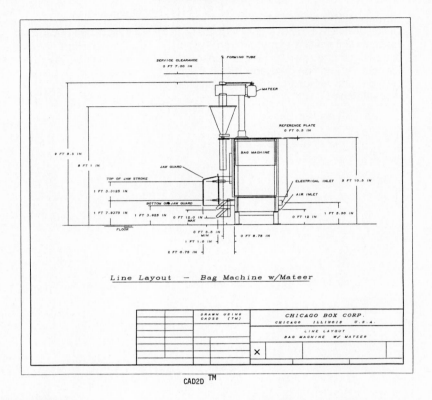

Line Layout — Bag Machine w/Mateer

CAD2D ™

CAD2D™ Computer-Aided Drafting and Design System

CAD2D is a software system for automated drafting, computer-aided design, management graphics, and manufacturing applications.

The methods and procedures for using CAD2D are directly analogous to the methods and procedures a drafter uses when preparing drawings on a drafting table using manual methods. CAD2D replaces all the drafter's triangles, T squares, drafting machines, templates, French curves, splines, lettering machines, pens, and stick-ons as well as his or her programmable calculator. It integrates all of these tools into a readily understandable and easy-to-use system for producing high-quality, precision drawings efficiently and economically.

In order to support a wide variety of application areas CAD2D is designed to interface to a variety of graphic display and input devices, as well as computer-driven plotters and other graphic output equipment.

The CAD2D user communicates with the system through mnemonic commands which are issued either by typing them on a keyboard or by picking them from one or several menus attached to a graphic input tablet. The commands are executed immediately and the results of the execution are displayed on the CRT screen. Menus can be interactively defined and redefined during a CAD2D operating session. Typing and other errors are recognized immediately and described on the CRT. User-defined procedures, termed Macros, may also be created, edited, debugged, and executed. Macros are treated in the same way as CAD2D system commands and are extremely useful for customizing the system for specific applications. Productivity may be improved by grouping frequently used command sequences into a single Macro.

Straight lines, multipointed straight lines, circles, partial circles, ellipses, partial ellipses, parametric cubic spline segments, and multipointed splines can be created. Coordinate data may be provided through the keyboard or from a graphic input device such as a graphic tablet. Input coordinates may be automatically translated to the nearest intersection on one of several user-defined grids or to coordinate points already in the data base.

Lines may be created with any desired pattern or width. Common patterns include dashed, centerline, phantom line, and dotted lines. Line width can be specified to offset and redraw a line up to 32 times. This technique can be used in lieu of a multiple-pen plotter to create a virtually limitless variety of line widths.

CAD2D generates high quality text in a variety of fonts under complete control of the user. The user can create text information and place it on the drawing in any location and orientation, at any size, slant, or aspect ratio, with any type of justification, and using any line width.

Merely by selecting the points between which a dimension is desired, the dimensioning commands create accurate, precisely located, correctly labeled dimensions. Any major and minor units (such as feet and inches) can be defined by name and scale factor. This capability allows drawings to be redimensioned in different units very quickly and easily. Also, arrow-tipped leaders with attached text may be created easily.

Since drawings are stored in on-line disk files and are immediately accessible, all editing and drawing changes are performed interactively using the CRT and graphics input tablet.

A new picture of the graphic data base may be viewed at any time on the CRT display terminal. The width and center of the viewing window may be controlled and the user may zoom in on a portion of the drawing or pan across the drawing quickly and easily. When a hard-copy drawing is desired, the plotting scale and window are specified and the plotter quickly creates a finished drawing. If multiple work stations are sharing a single plotter, the plot requests are placed in a queue and processed automatically on a first-come, first-served basis.

Along with the system commands, CAD2D provides a complete algebraic, relational, and logical expression evaluator, as well as a powerful procedure definition (Macro) facility. These two advanced capabilities are completely integrated into the CAD2D command language and provide very powerful, flexible, and easy-to-use functions.

The user interface to CAD2D is a command language with an easy-to-learn grammar and syntax. CAD2D commands have been designed to be simple and easy to learn. Since all of a user's needs cannot be anticipated, the system provides many simple, single-function commands. Operators can define more complex operations by creating new commands called Macros. Thus, the CAD2D language can be tailored and enhanced to meet new specific operator needs as they are identified.

❖MATRIX INSTRUMENTS INC.

Matrix Instruments Inc.
230 Pegasus Avenue
Northvale, NJ 07647
(201) 767-1750

Color Graphic Recorder
Model QCR™-D2000

The QCR camera system assembles images from information that is received directly from the CPU via an IEEE-488 interface. Therefore, by incorporating this digital computer software approach to color film recording, the QCR™-D2000 is not limited to the resolution of the color terminal and is able to produce images with a resolution of 2048 × 1366 pixels on 35 mm slides—images exposed through the QCR™-D2000 at a rate in excess of 15 frames/hour. The QCR™-D2000 combines simple operational procedures with stable, repeatable performance to provide extremely high quality color slides with no visible raster lines or jagged edges, even when large format projection is employed.

The QCR™-D2000 uses the film as a memory element, totally eliminating the need for a costly frame buffer and rendering the unit independent of the user's existing soft-copy capability. Crystal-controlled electronic timing and control circuitry are used throughout the unit, ensuring a high degree of repeatability in the creation of an image.

Color Graphic Recorder
Model 3000

Matrix Instruments' Color Graphic Recorder Model 3000 is a compact, desk-top, rack mountable, mobile camera system that records photographic hard copy from the output of raster scan terminals. The system, featuring battery back-up of memory, separate digital calibration of red, green, blue, brightness, contrast, and exposure with storage of eight separate calibration settings for each parameter, uses a multiple selection of interchangeable camera backs to produce 35 mm slides, 8 in× 10 in, 4 in× 5 in or SX-70 instant color prints, 8 in× 10 in transparencies, instant or otherwise, or 16 mm or 35 mm motion picture film.

The Model 3000 also provides switch-selectable multiple interlace, which can be used to eliminate raster lines in the recorded image. With dimensions of 10.5 in high, 16.5 in wide, 22 in deep, and a weight of 45 pounds, the Model 3000 furnishes high quality, precise, accurate color graphics in hard copy for various applications including business information graphics, computer-aided design and manufacturing, process control, remote sensing applications, cartography, digital image processing, and computer-animated motion pictures.

IVEGATEK

Megatek Corporation
3931 Sorrento Valley Boulevard
San Diego, CA 92191
(714) 455-5590

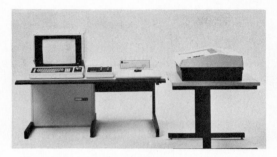

The Whizzard 7200 family offers line-drawing flexibility, speed, and operator-interaction capabilities. Connected to the host computer with a parallel interface, Whizzard 7200's can support multiple workstations with either stroke refresh or raster display monitors—or both. A proprietary 32-bit Graphics Engine™ processes 12-bit coordinate data to create a 4096^2 "virtual display space"—independent of the type of display. Coordinates, attributes, and graphic subroutines are stored in a 64K-byte display list memory, expandable to 192K bytes.

Whizzard 7210 is a full-refresh, high resolution stroke refresh display system. The basic configuration features an analog vector generator and a 21 in electromagnetic display with either a 10-mil or a 15-mil spot size.

Whizzard 7250 is a realtime, dynamic raster refresh graphics system. Hardware includes a digital vector generator, one or more double-buffered 512^2 or 1024^2 bit planes, and a dual-channel video output. The 19 in noninterlaced display can be either monochrome or coded in 16 colors selected from a palette of 4096.

Whizzard 7290 combines both calligraphic-stroke and dynamic color-raster in a single dual-display graphics system. Two separate vector generators, analog and digital, support the two display screens. Both are driven by the same graphics engine and draw from the same or different coordinate data stored in the Whizzard display-list memory.

The Whizzard 7600 family Included in all Whizzard 7600 family members is an Intel 8086-based local intelligent front end processor (LIFE™), a 3-D surface processor, Megatek's proprietary 32-bit microprocessor Graphics Engine™, and more than 512K bytes of usable RAM in addition to 192K bytes display list memory. All are linked by Megatek's dual bus architecture to increase user interaction through the system's intelligent peripherals.

Whizzard 7610—Stroke refresh display with 4096^2 screen resolution, monochromatic or beam penetration color output.

Whizzard 7640—Raster 512^2 resolution, monochromatic display.

Whizzard 7645—Raster 1024^2 resolution, monochromatic display.

Whizzard 7650—Raster 512^2 resolution, eight or 16 color display.

Whizzard 7655—Raster 1024^2 resolution, eight or 16 color display.

Whizzard 7690—Dual 4096^2 stroke and 512^2 raster display, combining 7610 and 7655 workstations.

Whizzard 7695—Dual stroke 4096^2 and 1024^2 raster display combining 7610 and 7655 workstations.
All systems can be interfaced with the host computer over unlimited distances by the RS-232 serial link or as far as 1,000 feet with the high-speed parallel IEEE-488 interface.

PERKIN-ELMER

Perkin-Elmer Corporation
Data Systems Group
2 Crescent Place
Oceanport, NJ 07757
(201) 870-4768

The CADAM® (Computer-Graphics Augmented Design and Manufacturing) system is an interactive, general purpose 3-D design and drafting system containing analytical design aids for use in design drafting, numerical control processing, and other engineering or manufacturing applications.

The new Perkin-Elmer Distributed CADAM Systems are designed to satisfy the needs of design and manufacturing firms requiring a cost-effective method of deploying CAD/CAM capabilities throughout their organizations.

Users of the new Perkin-Elmer systems have both the power and responsiveness of a local computer and access to the organization's centralized data base of drawing and design information.

The basic Perkin-Elmer product offering includes systems with one to four workstations of interactive graphic terminals and an 80 MB disk for local drawing storage. The system optionally includes hard copy plotting capabilities where users require quick-look or high quality drawings.

A single terminal workstation from Perkin-Elmer includes a Series 3200 supermini with 2MB of memory; high performance floating point processor; console terminal; 80 MB disk; a graphics terminal with keyboard, light pen, and function keys; and a user oriented worktable with chair. Options include 24 in and 36 in electrostatic plotters, magnetic tape, HASP telecommunications, and additional disk drives.

CADAM® is a registered trademark of CADAM, Inc., a subsidiary of Lockheed Corporation

Prime Computer, Inc.
Prime Park
Natick, MA 01760
(617) 655-8000

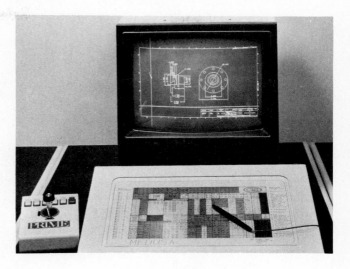

The Prime MEDUSA system is modularly designed.

Features of the Prime workstation include:

- Operation with MEDUSA™ computer-aided design software from Prime
- Raster scan technology
- Workstation includes: video processor, video display monitor, data tablet, joystick, and alphanumeric terminal
- High resolution, 1280 x 1024 pixel memory, 19-in monitor
- Graphics enhancements: circles, polygons, conics, fill algorithm, multiple line styles
- Intelligent workstation operation: pan/-zoom, selective erase
- Color video workstation or Monochrome video workstation

Monitor Specifications:
19-in display
Raster scan technology
1024 x 1024 resolution

Data Tablet
11-in x 17-in active area
Pen stylus with switch in tip
Video Processor Specifications:
Monochrome Video Processor (PW93)
  Memory plane—1
  Monitor refresh rate—50/60 Hertz
Color Video Processor (PW95)
  Memory planes—3
  Colors—8 out of possible 4096
  Monitor refresh rate—25/30 Hertz
Pan
  Zoom—X1, X2, X3 . . . X16
PW93 and PW95
  Serial interface, RS-232-C
  Video driver circuitry
  Graphics primitives
  Multiple line styles
  Line drawing
  Fill algorithm
  Selective erase
  Cursor control—read/position cursor control
  Write complement
  Joystick interface

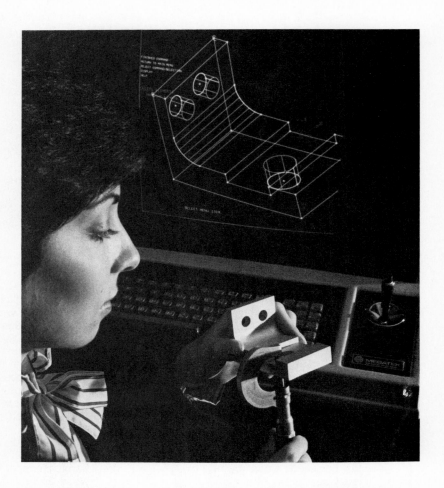

SPERRY⬩UNIVAC

Sperry Univac
P.O. Box 500
Blue Bell, PA 19424
(215) 542-4213/4218

The UNISCAD system is a simple, easy-to-use system, which aids productivity at every step and minimizes the training required for an experienced professional to use the system effectively. Security and integrity of the design data base can be protected electronically with the UNISCAD system. Access to drawings can be restricted on the basis of passwords.

The system is composed of four primary modules—Design, Engineering Analysis, Drafting, and Numerical Control. The key Design module allows users to define parts and combine them to form assemblies and products. For added flexibility, the UNISCAD system has solids modeling capabilities, allowing the user to build complex designs from simple primitive solids.

Summagraphics Corporation
35 Brentwood Avenue
P.O. Box 781
Fairfield, CT 06430
(203) 384-1344

Summadraft Design Drafting System (Single- and Dual-User Versions)

The Summadraft Design Drafting System is an advanced low-cost computer-aided design/drafting (CAD) system intended for use where heavy volumes or the need for increased operational flexibility require greater capacity and faster speeds than are available from Summagraphics' standard Datagrid II system. It includes both hardware and software.

Also available is a dual-user Summadraft system incorporating two workstations. The dual-station version permits two persons to use the system simultaneously without it being appar-ent to either that somebody else is on-line. To accomplish the response speed required, a 128K byte central processor is provided. Both workstations have graphic and alphanumeric CRT's and digitizers.

The Hardware
Incorporated in the Summadraft system are two displays—a 19-in storage tube for graphic output and an alphanumeric CRT with keyboard. Optional raster displays, including a color display, are available. Such raster displays permit selective erasure and the instantaneous correction of a portion of a drawing, adding to the speed and productivity of the system. The central processor is capable of supporting 128K bytes of random-access memory (RAM). The integral hard disk pro-

---

vides storage for 12.5 megabytes of symbol and drawing files. A floppy disk drive provides for 1.26 megabytes of removable storage, which can be used for off-line drawing storage or for other purposes.

Geometric Constructions in which lines, arcs, circles, rectangles, polygons, parabolas as well as fillets, cutouts, and splines are automatically constructed and oriented either by digitizing two or three points or by mathematical construction initiated by touching a symbol on a menu.

Geometric Definition and Calculation wherein such parameters as lengths, areas, angles are automatically calculated from interactive graphic inputs. The system also can perform calculations of parenthetic equations at any time during the design session.

File Management enabling the orderly filing and retrieval of drawings and symbols. Part of the file management system is the ability to create "State" files. These files store and re-create all system parameters such as alignment, type fonts, and pen types under which a drawing was originally created. This reduces set-up times for similar drawings in the future.

Display Commands including enlargement of drawings on the graphic CRT for detail work or reduction for overall viewing; *TEXT ON/OFF* which permits viewing the drawing with or without text, and *LAYERING* which permits the selective and simultaneous viewing of as many as 255 different "overlays" as, for example, in creating multi-layer printed circuits or in viewing electrical, piping, ducting, or other systems in a building layout.

**T&W
SYSTEMS,
INC.©**

T & W Systems, Inc.
18437 Mt. Langley
Fountain Valley, CA 92708
(714) 963-3913

T-Square and CAD Apple
General Purpose Drafting

User friendly, easy to learn.
Four input modes.
Up to 63 levels.
Two different types of the "snap to" function.
*Windows are defined in terms of real world
    coordinates.*
*Grids are defined in terms of real world coordi-
    nates.*
*The user can define all "Default" values (i.e.
    text height, base window . . .) and
    "Switches" (i.e. show coordinates, turn on
    this level, . . .).*
Workfile recovery.
"Help" feature.
Auto dimensioning.

System Description
Here are a few of the features of the
T-SQUARE system.

The Computer
The computer used is the monochrome or
color TERAK based on DEC's LSI-11, 16 bit
word microcomputer with hardware floating
point and up to 256K bytes of double ported
dynamic MOS RAM memory.

Mass Memory
One or two dual density flexible disk drives
with head life over 15,000 hours. 40 MB Winchester drives optionally available.

Display
The video controller is designed to provide
medium resolution (320 by 240 dots monochrome or 640 by 480 color) displays very
quickly for checking a design before allowing it
to be drawn on the plotter.

Digitizer
Several digitizers are available as peripherals
including 11 in by 11 in with 200 lines per inch
resolution up to large table-sized digitizers.

Plotter
A number of 11 in by 17 in plotters or 22 in
and 36 in wide drum plotters are available to
provide quality drawings.

Printer
Several matrix printers are available as an
option.

Software
All application software is written in PASCAL
and runs under the control of the UCSD
PASCAL operating system.

Tektronix, Inc.
P.O. Box 500
Beaverton, OR 97077
(503) 685-3043/3907

The drafting software runs on a Tektronix 4054 Graphics Computer. A complete configuration of Tektronix software and supporting hardware includes a desktop computer with a 19-inch DVST screen and dynamic graphics memory, over 1.8 megabytes of floppy disk storage, a 20″ by 20″ graphics input tablet, and the 2-D drafting software. The system can also support most CalComp plotters. A color-enhanced DVST screen and 36 in by 48 in tablet is optionally available.

The Tektronix package provides flexibility to accommodate different drafting standards, and gives users alternative ways to accomplish drafting tasks. For example, the package provides 15 ways to input lines, arcs, and circles, 10 different annotation methods, and 6 ways to temporarily blank out sections of a drawing for ease in editing. The package permits use of either grids or construction lines to help precisely orient drawing features. The package complies with ANSI Y14 drafting standards. Use of Graphic Model Exchange (GMX) file format allows users to exchange graphic data between the drafting package and other Tektronix software including the PLOT 50 Picture Composition and Interactive Digitizing packages. A variety of other PLOT 50 Software packages are available for graphics applications.

The package includes features common to quality drafting software. For example, the package allows a user to draw symbols and repeatedly use them in a drawing or a series of drawings. A user can also delete unwanted items in any of several ways or replace symbols of one type with symbols of another type. One can stretch items or enlarge details with a window function. Users can create or revise drawings on up to 127 levels. This will, for example, allow a user to draw the wall of a building on one level, plumbing to another, and the electrical wiring on a third level.

Terak Corporation
14151 North 76th Street
Scottsdale, AZ 85260
(602) 998-4800

Model 6124 Minn Draft

Combining two programs, DRAW and DRAFT, Minn Draft allows a student to describe simple, three-dimensional objects in algebraic terms by assigning X, Y, and Z coordinates to every vertex. Any errors in mathematical description become apparent when viewed in the three dimensions. Once the object is successfully defined, it can be rotated to any desired view including each of the standard projections typically seen on an engineering drawing, or into an auxiliary projection such as isometric.

Draw Program

The DRAW program allows the user to draw and view simple three-dimensional wire-frame objects from any angle. Objects are constructed out of two basic primitives—points and lines. User input is limited to X, Y, and Z coordinates for each corner of the object to be drawn. Lines are defined by specifying the beginning and endpoint number of the line. The input process is guided by a series of explicit prompts with forgiving error messages for any typing error that might occur.

There are two main options to the program:

DATA: Erases the screen and presents the user with a menu of different input options from which to choose.

VIEWS: Erases the screen and presents the user with a menu of different output options.

Draft Program

The DRAFT program turns the Terak Graphics Computer into a computer-aided design (CAD) work station. It supports command menu selections and input from a digitizer tablet as well as from the keyboard. With a plotter it supplies high quality drawings as final output. These added capabilities provide the Terak system with the necessary versatility to function as an industrial quality CAD station.

Terak Minn Draft Features

- Three dimensional data base.
- Five overlay layers.
- Semiautomatic dimensioning (linear and circular).
- Zoom-in/zoom-out window control.
- Menu driven for ease of operation.
- Keyboard/cursor/digitizer input modes.
- B size drawing output.

Drafting Entities Include

- Point.
- Line (horizontal, vertical, point-to-point, and chained).
- Circles and arcs.
- Text.
- Leader.
- Dimensioning (linear and circular).

Vector Automation, Inc.
Village of Cross Keys
Baltimore, MD 21210
(301) 433-4202

The drafter/designer uses a natural dialogue to "talk" to the CADMAX-I via the data tablet and keyboard. He or she instructs the CADMAX-I to create, scale, rotate, modify, and/or label the various elements of the design or drawing.

The CADMAX-I "answers" by interpreting the instructions, accomplishing what it was directed to do, displaying the results on the terminal CRT screen, and compiling a data file corresponding to the drawing produced and displayed.

When the "drafting effort" is complete, the data file corresponding to the drawing con-structed, is stored on a hard disk for perma-nent storage. The stored data file can be "copied" to recall a drawing for modification—or to produce an inked, hard copy on a plot-ter. In addition, the data file can be copied onto a magnetic cartridge unit for archival stor-age, to provide "safe copy" backup.

Features
- **Instantaneous Response**—displayed pic-ture is always up-to-date.
- **Simultaneous Design and Plot**—through use of multi-tasking operating system.
- **Geometric Construction Tool**—automati-

cally provides a visual method of indicating computed locations.

- **Associative Data Base**—keeps track of connections between various drawing elements.
- **Vertically Integrated System**—Both hardware and software are designed as a "unit" to provide optimum CAD/CAM system performance.
- **Model Accurate Data Base**—all coordinate data stored in floating point format.

GRAPHICS WORKSTATION—VECTOR AUTOMATION, INC.

Graphic Terminal—21 in vector stroke refresh with 4096 × 4096 resolution.
Keyboard—separate, standard 95-key ASCII for text entry.
Graphics Processor—high performance minicomputer with bipolar bit slice technology.

Data Tablet—11 in × 11 in active surface for all drafting commands.
Workstation Table

WINCHESTER DISK STORAGE
Provides on-line storage of designs and drawings constructed.

MAGNETIC TAPE CARTRIDGE UNIT
Provides a duplicate set of drawing files—for backup, to install software, and to communicate drawings between CADMAX-I systems.

PLOTTER (optional)
Produces up to D size, multi-color ink drawings on paper, vellum, or mylar.

DIGITIZER (optional)
Drawings already in existence can be readily digitized and incorporated into CADMAX-I storage.

VERSATEC
A XEROX COMPANY

Versatec Co.
2805 Bowers Avenue
Santa Clara, CA 95051
(408) 988-2800

Converting Vectors to Rasters

Typically, drawing data is developed as a series of raster scans across the paper width. Plotting is raster format is much faster than moving a pen from vector to vector, but it does require vector-to-raster conversion.

Ordered vectors can be converted to raster data by Versatec hardware or software. For example, minicomputer users can choose a rack-mounted Vector-to-Raster Converter to perform the conversion with their own computer and Versaplot software IBM 360 and 370 users can perform this function with on-line, off-line, and remote Versatec vector processing equipment or do the job on their IBM computer. When vector processing hardware is used, Versaplot simply outputs ordered vectors directly to the equipment.

Problems

1. Select one manufacturer listed in this chapter with whom you are not familiar. Prepare and send a letter requesting product information. Once the information has been received, write a description that includes the following points:

   a. Determine if the system is micro, mini, or mainframe.
   b. Determine the system capacity.
   c. List the pieces of equipment.
   d. List the features of this system.
   e. Include the cost of the system.

APPENDIX I
Line Generation Using a Graphics Tablet[1]

Step 1: Start up system

A. This Tektronix system uses a single screen. All instructions, prompts, and graphics are displayed on one storage tube.

B. If peripheral equipment is used, it must be first turned on. In this case, a graphics tablet must be used. It is activated by a switch located on the rear panel of the console (refer to Fig. 3-1). If a disk were to be used, the disk drive unit would also have to be turned on. The switch location is on the front panel.

C. Next, turn on the computer. The switch, located under the right of the keyboard, prevents accidental power loss.

Tektronix desktop computer.

[1] Courtesy Tektronix, Inc.

Step 2: Insert software

A. Select the appropriate disk or tape. A tape may be inserted in a slot located on the terminal as illustrated. A disk must be inserted into the disk drive slot.

B. If a tape is used, no further instruction is required. For the disk, additional instructions are required. Refer to the Tektronix manual for specifics.

Insert tape.

File manager.

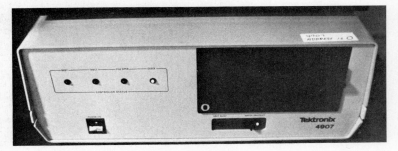

Step 3: Load the program

A. Using a tape, press the AUTO-LOAD button on the keyboard. A directory of the stored programs will appear on the screen as illustrated.

B. Call up the desired program, in this case, DRAFTING DIGITIZER. This is accomplished by first pressing key 2 on the alphanumeric.

C. Next, press Return (for carriage return). The program will be selected.

Directory.

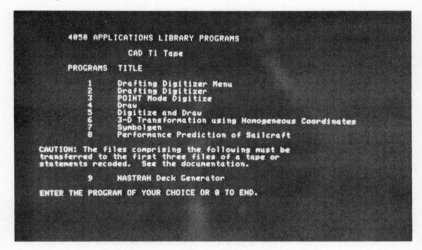

Pressing key 2.

Step 4: Set drawing surface

A. The menu and rough sketch must first be placed on the tablet. Locate the lower left corner of the drawing approximately 2 in up and 2 in to the right. This is the origin.

B. The console (refer to Fig. 2-19) must be set in the POINT mode. This may be accomplished by pressing the POINT button.

C. Set the drawing origin as follows:
1. Press the ORIGIN button on the control console and hold.
2. Place the tip of the stylus at the origin.
3. Press the stylus and hold.
4. Release the ORIGIN button and stylus.
5. Press Return on the alphanumeric.

D. Set the surface area of the sketch to be digitized. Follow the instructions on the screen as illustrated.

Graphics tablet, stylus, and menu.

Stylus at origin and press console button.

Instructions to set drawing surface area.

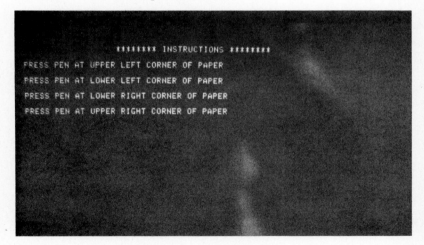

Step 5: Locate line endpoints

A. Locate the stylus at the first endpoint of the line to be drawn. Press it down. This digitizes the first point.

B. Locate the stylus at the second endpoint. Press it on the desired location. This digitizes the second point. The points are displayed on the screen as illustrated.

First endpoint displayed.

Both endpoints displayed.

Step 6: Drawing a line

A. Select the LINE menu item on the graphics tablet. Locate the tip of the stylus any place within the area of the box marked LINE. Press the stylus to digitize this selection. A line is immediately displayed on the CRT. It will be located between the two digitized points.

B. You may add lines on the screen by repeating Steps 5 and 6. The lines may be object, hidden, or center type. Simply select the appropriate menu item. This method may be used to rapidly convert a rough sketch into a finished drawing. See Appendix IV.

Selecting line menu.

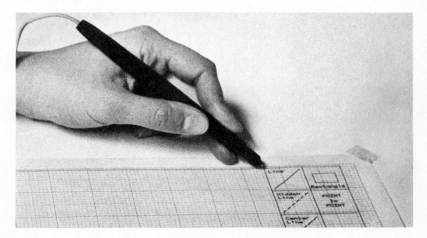

Line display on a CRT.

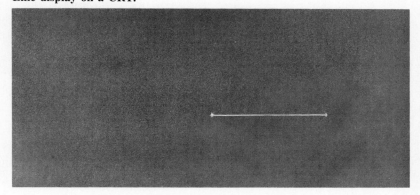

APPENDIX II
Line Generation Using a Light Pen[1]

Step 1: Start a drawing

A. The system is up. This means that it is activated. A FILES listing appears on the screen.

B. Use the light pen to select an appropriate user file. This is done by pressing the pen against the desired text.

Files on the screen.

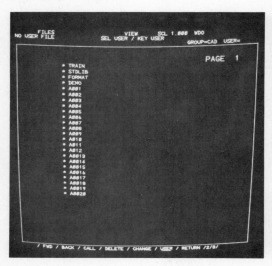

File selection.

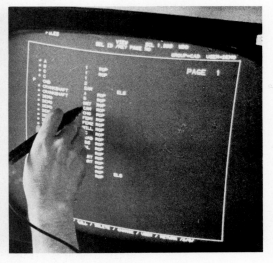

Step 2: Locate line endpoints

A. CADAM is a large, mainframe system. Thus, many options are available for creating lines. The method of

[1] Courtesy CADAM, which is a registered trademark of CADAM, Inc.

using established points on the screen is used here. The points will be used to establish a reference (endpoint).

Press the POINT button on the function keyboard. (CADAM prefers the term *function keyboard* to the term *function board*.) The system is now in the POINT mode. This will be indicated at the upper left corner of the screen.

B. Press the light pen to any desired location on the screen. A point will appear. This may be done for additional points.

Function keyboard.

Light pen selecting a point.

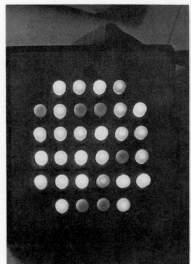 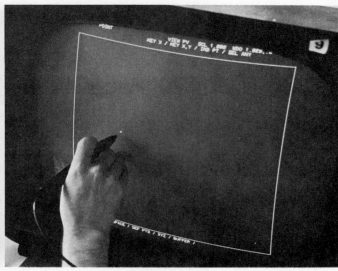

Step 3: Select the line type

A. Press the LINE button on the function keyboard. The system is now in the LINE mode. This will be indicated at the upper left corner of the screen.

B. Select the type of line from the menu across the bottom of the screen by pressing the light pen against the word HORIZ. This means horizontal lines will be drawn.

C. Next, press the pen against the menu item LENGTH. This means that the length of the line may now be selected.

Light pen selecting a horizontal line.

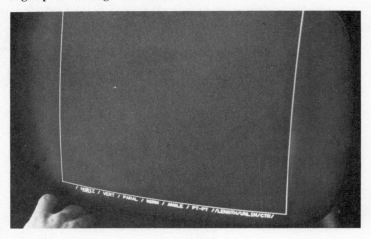

Step 4: Select the point method

A. The method of drawing the line is the next part of this procedure. A choice of methods, known as message options, appears across the upper right of the screen. Select the point method. Do this by pressing the pen against the SEL PT.

B. Choose the desired first endpoint using the light pen.

CRT message options.

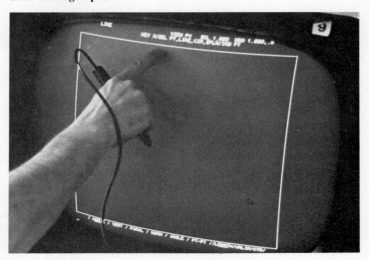

Light pen selecting a point.

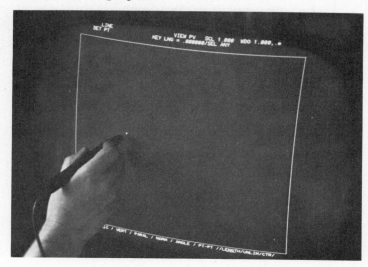

Step 5: Select the line length

A. The message options change. A request to key in a length appears at the upper right.

B. Key in the desired length (e.g., 5) using the alphanumeric.

C. Press the End key on the alphanumeric.

Message option showing length request.

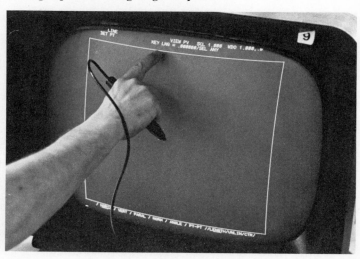

Keyboard length entry.

Step 6: Draw a line

A. Use the light pen to determine the direction of the horizontal line. (For example, move the pen to the right side of the point.) Press the pen to the screen.

B. While pressing the pen to the screen, press the INDICATE button on the function keyboard. The line will appear on the screen.

Press the INDICATE button on the function keyboard.

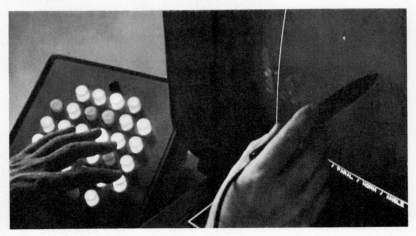

Line display on the CRT.

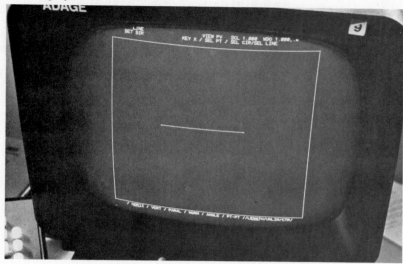

Step 7: Draw additional lines

A. You may add horizontal lines (to the same length) on the screen by repeating Step 6.

B. If other types of lines (vertical, etc.) are desired, return to Step 3 and repeat Steps 3, 4, 5, and 6.

Lines on the CRT.

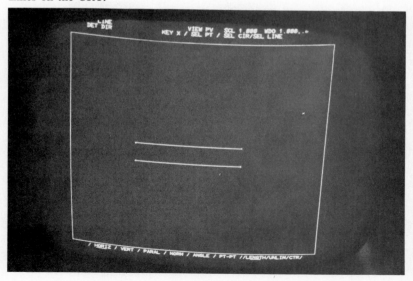

APPENDIX III
Circle Generation
Using a Menu Pad[1]

Step 1: Start up system

A. The Bausch & Lomb system utilizes dual screens. The screen shown at the left is used for facilitation purposes. All instructions, messages, cues, and prompts are displayed on this screen.

B. The screen shown at the right is for the drawing display. It consists of a storage-tube type of CRT.

C. To activate the system, turn on the main power switch.

Dual screen setup.

[1]Courtesy Bausch & Lomb Inc.

Step 2: Select menu pad

A. Each function is located on a menu pad. This is similar to a function board except selection is made with a puck. Actually, the digitizing process is involved here.

B. The drawing size may first be loaded before execution. Do this by selecting the appropriate DRAWING BORDER or DISPLAY DRAWING SIZE with the puck.

C. The upper right side of the pad has a variable menu. It may be used to place any type of symbol (i.e., piping, electrical, etc.) on the screen. Each menu is a separate overlay consisting of 20 symbols. Any of eight menus (160 figures) may be called up. This is referred to as menu switching. Simply select the LOAD MENU number located below this overlay section.

Menu pad and puck.

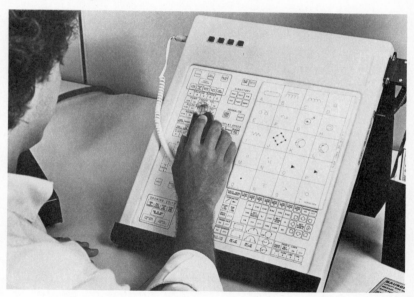

Step 3: Select circle

A. Three types of circles can be selected from the menu pad. These include:

    1. Three points on the circumference not in a straight line.

2. The center of the circle and one point on the circumference.

3. Two points on the circumference corresponding to the circle diameter.

B. With the puck, select the desired type of circle (e.g., type 2—the center and radius). This is done by placing the puck cross hair within the rectangle. Depress the button on the puck. The type of circle has been selected and will remain selected until you quit the function.

Functions on the menu.

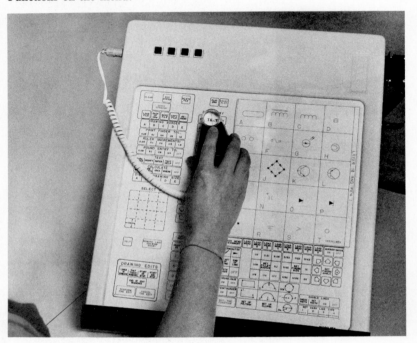

Step 4: Locate center of circle

A. Move the horizontal and vertical cross hairs (cursor) on the screen to the desired location. Use the thumbwheels located on the right side of the alphanumeric keyboard. The horizontal wheel moves the horizontal line. The vertical wheel moves the vertical line. The location of the cross-hair intersection defines the center point.

B. Numeric keys 2 and 3 on the alphanumeric interactive keyboard are used to determine the location of the center. Key 2 is pressed if an object line circle is desired. Key 3 is pressed if a hidden line circle is desired.

Keyboard and thumbwheels.

Step 5: Locate circumference

A. Pressing key 2 instructs that a solid object line circle be drawn. The intersection of the crosshairs will flash bright on the screen. This is a nonpermanent condition to be used as reference. It is referred to as a *point marker*.

B. Next, repeat Step 4, visually locating the circle radius.

Center of circle at intersection of cross hair.

Step 6: Draw the circle

A. Press alphanumeric key 2. A solid line circle will appear on the screen.

First circle drawn.

Step 7: Locate a second circle

A. A second circle can be drawn concentric with the original center.
    1. Repeat Step 4, by first returning the cross hairs to the original center.

B. It is difficult to locate the exact center. Thus, after manipulating the cursor to get it as close as possible to the center, press alphanumeric key 8. The exact center will be located (within a specified tolerance).

C. Repeat Step 5, except press key 3 for a hidden line command.

Cursor placement at second circle circumference.

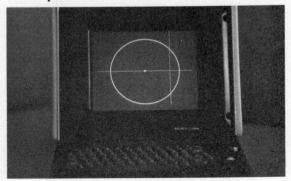

Step 8: Draw the second circle

A. Press alphanumeric key 3. A hidden line circle will appear on the screen.

B. Additional circles may be drawn by this method. The user must exit this function before executing other functions. This is done by pressing QUIT THE FUNCTION with the puck.

C. Additional functions can be executed by the selection of any other geometric function. The other methods to draw a circle, for example, may be selected from the menu pad.

Second circle drawn.

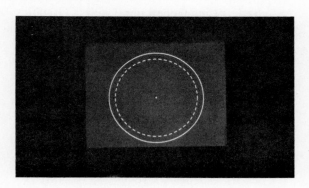

APPENDIX IV
Piping Schematic Using a Graphics Tablet[1]

Step 1: Locate line endpoints

A graphics tablet may be used to quickly convert a rough sketch into a finished drawing. The sketch used in this example is a piping spool diagram (isometric). Appendix IV is a continuation of Appendix I, "Line Generation Using a Graphics Tablet." Continue to digitize line endpoints using the method given in Appendix I.

Point digitizing.

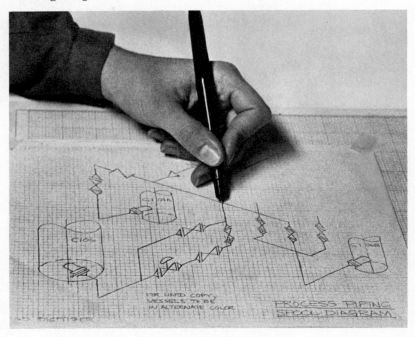

[1] Courtesy Tektronix, Inc.

Step 2: Display lines

Each time line endpoints and the LINE menu have been digitized, a line will be displayed on the screen. (Note: a program requiring a function board might be used. In this event, the appropriate button must be pressed for each line display.)

Partial display.

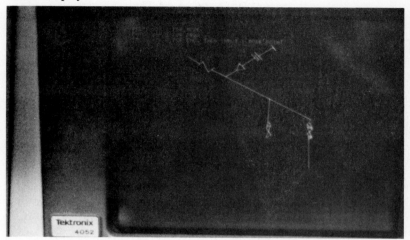

Step 3: Complete digitizing

Continue to digitize until the diagram is completed.

Digitizing final points.

Step 4: Produce a drawing

The drawing may be produced by either of the following methods, depending on the program used. The pen will reproduce the screen image on drafting media.

    A. Key in the instruction on the alphanumeric, or

    B. Press the button PLOTTER OUTPUT on the function board (user definable keys) located at the upper left of the terminal.

Drawing on plotter.

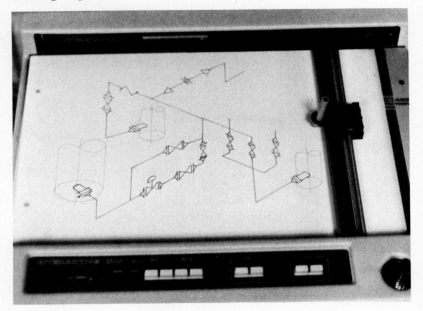

GLOSSARY

A
Ampere. Unit of electrical current. One ampere will flow through one ohm resistance at one volt potential difference.

Alphanumeric keyboard
A keyboard similar to the typewriter keyboard. Allows the user to input letter (alpha) and number (numeric) instructions to the central processor.

Ambient lighting
The surrounding level of lighting. It is much lower in CAD area than a traditional drafting room.

ANSI
American National Standards Institute. They have recommended drafting standards for all technical fields.

ASCII
American Standard Code for Information Interchange. Pronounced ''ask´ee'', it is an eight-level code for data developed by the American National Standards Institute (ANSI). It ensures compatibility between data services.

Automation
Equipment that increases productivity without additional expenditure of human energy.

AWG
American wire gage. A standardized series of wire conductor diameters. A no. 14 gage is the commercial minimum size allowed.

Axis
Distance from one side of an ellipse or arc to the opposite side 180° apart. There is a *major axis* and a *minor axis*.

Axonometric
A graphical representation that expresses three faces of an object. The faces are inclined to the plane of projection. The length, height, and depth are shown but not in perspective.

Baud
Data transmission rate of one bit per second.

Binary
The base 2 numbering system. Uses only the digits 0 and 1.

Bit
Taken from *b*inary dig*it*. It is a 0 or 1 signal.

Buffer
A short-time electronic storage device. It adjusts for a difference in the rate informa-

	tion flows when transmitting from one device to another. It is sometimes referred to as memory or internal storage.
Byte	A sequence of binary digits (bits) that the computer operates on as a single unit. It is eight bits and is the basis of comparison used in describing various systems and manufacturers. One byte is a character of memory. A megabyte would be 1 million characters.
CAD	Computer-aided drafting or computer-aided design and drafting.
CADD	Computer-aided design drafting or computer-aided design and drafting.
CAM	Computer-aided manufacturing.
Capacitor	An electrical device used to store energy and permit the flow of alternating current. Normally, designated C.
Carriage return	The carriage return on a typewriter keyboard corresponds to the end or return on a CAD alphanumeric.
Character	The coded symbol of a digit, letter, special symbol, or control function. The term *byte* is sometimes used to describe a character.
Chip	A small slice of material (such as silicon) containing electronic devices (transistors, diodes, resistors, and/or capacitors) which perform functions within a computer.
Chip technology	The use of small silicon chips for a central processing unit and storage memory.
Command	A series of directions used to execute a function on a CAD system.
Computer	Popular name referring to the CPU. It additionally includes the graphic display station and alphanumeric keyboard on small systems.
Concentric	Having a common center such as a circle or ellipse.
CPU	Central processing unit. The microprocessor portion of the computer that accomplished the logical processing of data. It contains the arithmetic, logic, and control circuits, and possibly the memory storage.
Cross-hatching	Section lining indicating that the surface has

been cut. Section lines usually consist of inclined, thin parallel lines. If there are different line patterns, they will indicate different materials. ANSI now uses cast iron hatching for all materials.

CRT
Cathode ray tube. Similar to a television screen, this screen allows the production of a drawing (visual display) without the use of vellum or Mylar.

Current
The rate or amount of electricity flowing. It is measured in units of amperes.

Cursor
The bright mark on the CRT that moves and locates positions on the screen. May be variously shaped (dot, crosshair, check, and so on).

Data processing
The use of computers to gather, manipulate, summarize, and report information that flows through an organization.

Dedicated
Used with a single terminal by one user. Said of a microprocessor generally used for one type of work. A dedicated system stands alone and does not hook in to any larger computer to complete work.

Default
The system automatically returns to one function type. Normally, it is the most common one. The default for line generation, for example, would be a solid line.

Desk-top computer
A dedicated computer small enough to be located on the user's desk.

Diagram
A drawing made up a series of symbols. These are usually not drawn to scale.

Digitizer
A term commonly used to describe a graphics tablet.

Digitizing
The method by which data is entered on a graphics tablet. A stylus or puck is "touched down" at a particular location. This touching down is called digitizing.

Diskette
Another name for a disk. It is a plastic-like (Mylar film) disk enclosed in a protective folder. Information is stored on a diskette.

Display
Visual output as seen on the screen of a CRT. It may be a drawing or alphanumeric data.

Dot matrix
A group of closely spaced dots with a

	printed pattern that looks like the shape of the desired character.
Dual display	The use of two CRTs. One screen is used for drawing preparation. The other for instructions and prompting.
Dump	Converting information from one medium to a different type of medium.
Fiber optics	Glass-like thin tubes that transmit a light source. The light source can be curved during transmission.
Firmware	Instructions that have been permanently placed into memory in a piece of equipment.
Floppy disk	A thin, flexible (nonrigid) disk that stores programs.
Font	A certain style and size of type.
Function	Produce a change in the display on a CRT screen. For example, adding a line or text.
Function board	A keyboard that allows for graphic data entry of various functions; for example, pressing a LINE program button will allow the input of a line onto the CRT.
Geometry modifier or manipulator	A function used to alter a drawing on the CRT screen. For example, shortening the length of a line is considered a geometry modifier or manipulator.
Graphic display station	The unit that displays the image or drawing. The most popular graphic display stations are CRTs.
Graphic tablet	An input device having a flat surface on which the work is done. A stylus or a puck is used for the graphical data entry. Information is transmitted to the CRT by means of an electrically controlled grid beneath the tablet's surface.
Grid	Bright dots on the CRT screen spaced to form a square pattern.
Hard copy	A preliminary drawing that is produced by the hard copy unit and is often used as a checkprint.

Hardware	Each piece of physical equipment is considered hardware.
Host	One central place where the data resides.
IC	Integrated circuit. See *Chip*.
Increment	See *Step*.
Ink jet	Shapes are formed by electrostatically spraying a fine stream of ink onto paper.
Input	Getting data into the information processing system.
Interactive	Refers to the need for a human to initiate communication between different parts of a computer system.
Intersection	The point at which two lines meet. For example, the crossing of two center lines is the intersection that defines the center of a circle.
Isometric	A view showing three visible faces of a cube that appear equal in shape and size. The side faces are at an angle of 30° to the horizontal.
Joystick	An input device which directly controls the cursor. The stick is moved in the same direction as the user wishes the cursor to move on the screen.
Light pen	An input pointing device. Data entry may be made directly onto the screen by positioning and activating the tip of the pen at the desired location.
Magnetic tape	Plastic-like (Mylar) film on which information may be stored.
Mainframe	A CPU utilized with many terminals for multipurpose use.
Mask	An interchangeable sheet often made of plastic. It fits over a function board, menu pad, or graphics tablet.
Medium	A drawing material that can normally be reproduced. Vellum and Mylar (thin plastic film) are the most popular.

Memory	Stored information, programs, and data inside automated equipment. One byte is a character of memory.
Menu	A selection from which the designer or drafter can choose various functions.
Menu pad	Also known as a menu tablet. An input device having a flat surface on which functions are selected using a stylus or puck. Similar to a function board without buttons.
Menu switching	Changing the available functions that can be executed on the CRT. A corresponding card is also changed. The interchangeable mask may be placed over a function keyboard, menu pad, or graphics tablet.
Micro	The smallest type of CAD system. Micros are dedicated units like home computers.
Microprocessor	The central processing unit of a microcomputer.
Mini	A CAD system having capabilities between a micro and a mainframe. Minis are generally dedicated for the specific purpose of the user. This type of CAD system is commonly used in industry.
mm	Millimeter. A metric term used to describe length. *Milli* refers to 0.001 (one-thousandth). One thousand millimeters are in a meter. Approximately 25.4 mm equal 1 in.
Mode	A part of a computer that allows the user to perform a certain type of function as: *point mode*.
Modem	Telephone translation of computer pulses used for long-distance graphic data transfer.
Mylar	A durable, long lasting polyester film used for the preparation of drawings. *Mylar* is a trade name. The product is made by Keuffel and Esser.
NC	Numerical control. The use of computer-generated instructions to manufacture a part.
NPN	Designation for the type of transistor known as *negative-positive-negative*.
Ohm	An ohm is the unit of resistance.

Operator	A general term for CAD users. Not all users are designers and drafters. A designer or drafter, however, may be an operator.
Output	The end result of what the system produces. Normally, this will be a hard copy.
PC	Printed circuit. An electronic assembly comprised of a nonconductive board, a conductive copper pattern, and electronic components.
Peripheral	Additional equipment working in conjunction with, but not as part of, the computer.
pF	Picofarad. A unit of measure equal to 10^{-12} farads. A *farad* is the unit of capacitance.
Plotter	An output device. A drawing of the screen display is automatically generated onto a plotter.
PNP	Designation for the type of transistor known as *positive-negative-positive*.
Power	The rate of expending energy. The unit watt (W) is used to describe electrical energy.
Processing unit (CPU)	The controlling unit of a computer system. It contains circuitry for logical decisions, arithmetic calculations, and a fixed amount of main storage.
Process piping	A category of design and drafting falling within the giant field of industrial plant design.
Program	A detailed set of coded instructions that are logically ordered. These are used for the operation of a computer.
Program button	Located on a function board. Pressing a button (e.g., LINE) connects the software program enabling that function (e.g., draw a line) to be performed.
Programmer	An individual who designs the sets of instructions, or programs, for the CAD system.
Q	Designation for a transistor. A transistor is a semiconductor usually made of silicon. It causes changes in current and voltage.

R	Designation for a resistor. A resistor is an electrical device used to oppose the flow of current.
RAM	Random access memory. Temporary memory: information can be written in or read out and lost when power is turned off.
Raster	A network or matrix of dots. Each dot falls within a square area known as a pixel.
Refresh	The method of redrawing each line of a graphic display.
Resolution	The number of addressable dots per unit area. Low-resolution screens produce jogged lines.
Robot	A system that simulates human activities from computer instruction.
ROM	Read-only memory. Permanent memory: information is stored permanently and is read out.
Scale ratio	The number which indicates how much larger or smaller the shape of an object is shown. For example, a 2 means that a drawing shows an object twice as large as actual.
Schematic	The arrangement of symbols and manner in which they are connected on a diagram.
Sepia	A translucent medium. If a translucent reproduction is made from an original, the reproduction also becomes reproducible.
Sequential access	A method of storage on external media in which information is stored one item after another. Tapes are sequentially accessed.
Software	The name given to programs that are input for the computer. The program gives instructions concerning the operational sequence.
Spline	A common term used to describe the irregular curve concept in conventional drafting.
Spool drawing	A three-dimensional isometric schematic diagram of a portion of a piping project.
Stand-alone	Similar to *dedicated*.
Step	A discrete function. A definite length or distance.

State of the art	Referring to the latest technical advancement.
Surface	Like a two-dimensional plane. It is an area having a thickness considered for practical purposes to be zero.
Symbol	An abbreviation; a code used to represent a component. Many national codes contain symbols. Once you learn the code, your ability to communicate ideas and information increases.
Terminal	Popular name given to the combination of a graphics display screen (CRT) and keyboard.
Three-dimensional view	A view of an object expressing its length, height, and depth. Also called 3-D.
Tilt	The angle at which an object is turned. It is normally measured in degrees.
Traditional drafter	A drafter not trained in CAD whose time is spent on traditional drafting techniques and tasks.
Translucent	Light can pass through. With reference to drafting media, the use of translucent material for drawings allows for reproducible prints.
Turnkey	The name given to a complete CAD system.
User	The individual who inputs data into, and receives information from, a CAD system.
User's manual	The procedures that apply to the specific manufacturer's equipment and programs.
V	Volt. The unit of electrical energy or potential.
Vector	Producing straight lines between two points.
Voice-activated	Systems that can recognize and respond to spoken words.
W	Watt. A unit of electrical power.
Winchester	A hard disk usually contained in a box-like unit. The unit rotates or drives the disk. Millions of characters of information may be stored on a Winchester disk.

Window	A visual display screen divided into one or more sections.
Wire frame	A series of thin wires connected to form a three-dimensional object.

INDEX